Suffolk

Essex

Mistley

Mistley Heath

Station Road

Bradfield

Bradfield Heath

Searching for Bessie

An Adventure in
Family History,
Poetry
and
Bessie's Recipes.

A story of a Mistley Riverside
Family 1881-2021

By Sheila Kelly

Searching for Bessie
by Sheila Kelly.

All illustrations from the authors collection © except pp.14 Copyright Dave Spicer and licensed for reuse under creativecommons.org/licenses/by-sa/2.0, pp. 16 © Petra McQueen and pp. 112 ©Peter Higginbotham / workhouses.org.uk by permission and pp.173 by Mandy Rose.

Typeset and book design by Dorian Kelly

A catalogue record for this book is available in the British Library.

ISBN 9-7-8099353349-5 softback

Publisher's Cataloguing-in-Publication data
Kelly, Sheila Elizabeth
Title of Book : Searching for Bessie / Sheila Kelly

The main category of the book - Biography
Other category: Family History
Other category: Poetry
Other category: Recipes

First Published June 2021 By
Guerilla Shakespeare Publishing
3 Gladstone Road. Colchester, UK
CO1 2EB
+44 (0)1206 798076
publisher@theatrearts.biz

Reason Family Tree
in 1939

m.1837

Samuel
Reason
1812-1893

Sarah
Jospall
1816-1893

William
Field
1827-1904

m.1860

Betsey
Pennifold
1840-1881

m.1891

George
Reason
1858-1935

Emily
Field
1868-

Bessie Emma
Reason
1894-1919

William
Aldridge
18--?

Ella Rose
Reason
1903-1916

m.1917

m.1931

m.1929

Joan Aldridge
Reason
1918-

Florence Emily
Reason
1891-

Neville
Sage
1890-

Millicent Dora
Reason
1898-

James
Kemp
1868-1936

Elsie Ida
Reason
1903-

Frank
Seager
1901-

George
Sage
1920 -

Irene
Sage
1921-

Evelyn
Sage
1923 -

George
Kemp
1931-

Eileen
Seager
1930 -

Valerie
Seager
1937-

About the Author

Sheila Kelly is proud to be an 'Essex Woman' from Colchester, raised among river estuaries, in a loving, resilient family. Now she enjoys being 'nana', mum, extra-mother, wife, cousin and friend in a diverse extended family. Once a daughter, (never a granddaughter) and niece, with great-aunts from Mistley, who told stories with echoes from long-ago, but not so far-away.

Sheila always wanted to "time-travel," and at six dug deep holes in her father's straight - rowed vegetable bed seeking for Roman remains. She still enjoys delving deep to find what the past was really like, and is still an eager "time-traveller."

Sheila reinvents herself often, from headteacher and clog-dancer, to Post-graduate Student at Cambridge University at 55, to children's integrative arts psychotherapist, to enthusiastic family historian, to first time author at 73; grateful to the NHS, also born in 1948, for support through breast cancer, and later spinal surgery. She takes "nothing for granted."

Varied life experiences are integrated to tell Sheila's family history (or her-story) exploring emotional, oral and social history, and left-overs in a new integrated approach. Family therapy reveals the emotional impact of one generation to the next, whilst narrative therapy explores how stories get distorted in retelling. As story-tellers and readers we bring our own stories and viewpoints so each will understand, interpret and retell the past differently.

"Searching for Bessie" binds family stories, recipes and memories; as a thank you to Sheila's ancestors, and a store cupboard for future generations. Hopefully readers might be tempted to retell their family stories in words or pictures, or re-make a family recipe, to reconsider past and future

Introduction:
Bessie, My Shadow Grandmother

All my cousins had grandmothers. I had none and was envious.
My questions were evaded. "They died long before you were born."

A curious child, I sought answers, and my great aunties, Flo, Millie and Elsie, were willing conspirators, "You look like your nana, Bessie, our dear sister...a cook in service...When your mother was a baby, Bessie had to bring her home after dark. Father was so ashamed of her."

Joan, my mother, resented Bessie, "She was killed in a bicycle accident, in 1919. I was only nine months old. An orphan and illegitimate. ..."

"No Auntie Elsie I don't want to see her photo." I secreted the photo.

Bessie was a constant shadow in our lives. My mother refused to speak about her, but was determined I would not follow in Bessie's footsteps.

I was raised strictly with tight rules, and watched carefully for any deviancy from Joan's determined path. But genes would out. Her perfect teenager became an adult rebel.

Later Auntie Millie passed on Bessie's hand written recipe book to my mother, which she even photocopied for me. It was a moment of acceptance.

Working with children, I saw the emotional impact of one generation on another, which can even alter genes. When I became a grandmother, I felt surges of new love, which made me more aware of the absence of Bessie in our lives. Writing my grandmothers' stories attempts to fill this gap, to find Bessie and myself. Bessie's mother Emily is central to this story, resilient and loving. A good mother to her five daughters, as well as her younger siblings, and later on to Joan, her orphaned granddaughter.

1: How to Find a Lost Family

Sit on the right hand side,

as the train departs Manningtree Station.

Turn back your watch to another time.

Listen, look, seek and search.

Past Railway Cottages, flooded roof-high

in 1953,

pigs and chickens swimming down Colchester Road.

Speed past wartime rail workers digging

dynamite out of the burning embankment.

Spot my mother, Joan, 90 years back

once a chattering confident child

swimming across Judas Gap,

Travel in and out of time.

Imagine,

wander away from yourself

Follow your gaze across the River Stour.

Drift through tidal ebb and flow,

mud banks, grass islands, river trickle,

high tide bluster, deep river mirror.

Swim through years to Mistley Walls.

Avoid flotsam from the bombed sewer.

Go past Wherry Corner and North House.

Over dead shells, frayed nets, sand castles.

To my family home, where sadly I never lived;

three riverside cottages, tied to the Maltings.

Frantic delivery wagons, shovel clatter,

towering silos, sticky smoked treacle scent.

Back to 1891, as my great grandparents move in.
Meet Emily, the gamekeeper's resilient daughter,
married to George, the ambitious foreman-maltster.
Daughters: Flo, Bessie, Millie, Elsie, and Ella arrived.
Five sisters brewed and bred by the riverside.

Pause in 1904, three anxious excited sisters
Flo, Bessie and Millie stare across the river,
at Buffalo Bill's circus train, while mother
Emily strains indoors, bearing twins.
Join the jolly Christmas crowd in 1960,
26 relatives for tea round the coffin table.
reading jokes in ill-fitting cracker hats.
Our family home through a century,
for birthdays, weddings and funerals.
Until 1993, when the last sister, Elsie died.
For me 'the sisters are all still there'

Meet Auntie Elsie at six on any Friday morning,
gentle, loving, smiling, sad with loss inside
cleaning intently, polishing her windows.
Find your reflection in her sparkling panes.

Next door, Auntie Flo brews tea on the kitchen range,welcoming,
wise, hard working, no frills.
This was my childhood Sunday retreat,

a family home to sustain my life voyage.
Acceptance, memories, love inwardly stored.

A family story I want to explore,
to delve into hidden, forgotten corners.
I search in photos, postcards, Ancestry,
records, newspapers to Find My Past.
Clues from my grandmother Bessie's
hand-written hundred year old recipe book,
from recipes for Green Tomato Pickle,
Queen of Puddings and Roman Pie.
I learnt from mothers and daughters
supportive in death, birth and love.

By weaving our family tales,
I hope to preserve our history,
my family and self entwined.
Word spun in complex patterns
with the odd dropped stitch
in a rag-rug meld of pre-loved scraps.
Read on to continue our travels
through space and time,
to discover my Riverside family
anchored on the banks of the Stour.

Or resume your journey to Ipswich.
Return to your stuffy train seat.
Rewind your watch to the correct time,
but beware of delays in reality
from dreams of past times.

Five Riverside Sisters outside the Maltings about 1912
L to R: Elsie, Bessie, Millie, Flo and Ella

2: Farewell to Horsted Keynes in 1881

Family stories are timeless, without a clear start and finish. For my great grandmother Emily Field, life began again in 1881.

Playground laughter, "Gee-up Emily, faster."
Piggybacked, Alfie ruled the world.
Emily, schoolmaster's nursery maid,
galloped indoors, high-chaired Alfie,
cut soldiers from fresh baked bread,
for dipping in top-shaved boiled egg.
Her perfect work, chosen from all the class.

Emily, distracted now, torn in half,
anxious about mother, weak at home,
caring for four day old twin brothers.
Father and siblings had moved away.
A wise gamekeeper, too insightful
about his tricky employer's stable fire.
Aware of insurance fraud,
forced to move to far away Essex.
Mother was to join her family,
after the birth of thriving twins,
Alfred and Frederick, the two Freds!
Emily, just 14, would not move.
Horsted Keynes was her home.

Mrs. Larter, schoolmaster's wife,
glided into her pristine kitchen,
her baby Frederick gently cradled.
"Emily you're needed at home
your mother has become unwell."

Emily sprinted through the graveyard,
shortcut between school and village.
Daffodils and primroses glowed orange,
mirroring the last rays of evening sun.
Emily's heart refused to 'with pleasure fill.'
She touched the white stone angel
guarding Flo's grave, her shadow sister,
Bed shared end to end, inseparable

but parted forever by diphtheria.
Emily whispered "I will stay with you.
I will not be dragged away to Essex."
Split, tugged in two. Family fragmented.
Emily skidded into Oddyne's cottage.
No greeting chatter, just subdued silence.
Stale unwashed nappies overflowed.
George, mouth ringed with damson jam,
sucked a crust of bread, eyes glazed,
alone in the kitchen, family disappeared.
Stove unlit, Emily shivered in the damp.
Usually mother baked, feeding countless
beaks of her chattering sparrow children,
listening to her girls' village gossip,
little brothers pushing wooden trains,
hooting in homage to the new railway.

Emily stretched out to cuddle George.
Weak kittens cried upstairs, "the twins".
Emily rushed up, patting George's curls.
Silent tears flowed down George's face.
'Even Em prefers those Fred babies.'
Toppled from his cradle, by not one
but two strangers.
He chewed, and cried.

Mother's bedroom smelt of oversweet lilies,
though flower less, airless, sad and muggy.
Mother was flushed, clammy, as Mary Ann
offered broth that, unswallowed, chin-dripped.
She whispered, "Get Nana, next door will go."
Mother tried to feed Freddie, he latched on,
sucked nothing, turned away and whined,
Hungry.

At ten, Jared's cart rumbled back, laden.
Painful silence broken by Nana and Aunt Rose.

Rose's milk flowed back, responding
to quiet screams from hungry nephews,
Alfred, wide eyed, gazed, chosen first,
his life path determined in a moment.
Smelt the sweet milk, homed in greedily.
Alfred guzzled, leaving none for his twin.
Freddie wailed, rejected another empty breast,
Emily dripped sugar water in his hungry beak.
Freddie ejected from the nest by his cuckoo twin.
Mother turned away, too drained to cry
'A failure, unable to suckle my babies.'
Isolated, missing strong, loving, William.
far away, unable to meet his twin sons.
Other births, he garden hovered,
digging twice-turned vegetable beds,
polished boots.
On constant watch,
until he rushed upstairs at the first cry.

Betsey wanted her new sons baptised.
At morning service on Sunday May 8th,
Pennifolds and Fields christened both Freds.
No parents present,
mother Betsey too ill, father in Essex,
but loving godparents prayed,
tried to dispel the encircling demons.
Sunlight streamed through stained glass,
rainbow danced on whitewashed walls.
Rose clutched contented Alfred close to her,
Emily rocked Frederick, crying, thrashing
stiffening in pain, racked by colic.
After the subdued Christening tea,
one by one, two by two, the family
visited Betsey upstairs, to say farewell.
Betsey held Alfred tight for the last time,
squeezing in love, with fading strength.
"Rose, please feed and mother Alfred."

10

Twin brothers parted, rarely to meet.
Downstairs the family whispered in corners.
Emily could smell the worry, overheard
"Send for William."
Emily poured sweet, milky tea for Mother.
Betsey stroked her face, as they sat, in peace.
"I'll see Flo again, and look after her.
Care for Freddie and my little ones.
Aunt Rose will raise little Alfred".
William arrived just in time, shocked,
rushed upstairs in his bowler hat.
Betsey laughed at her proud husband,
and fell into their last embrace.
William held her throughout the night.

Betsey was buried on 18th May 1881 at Horsted Keynes

Emily buried her loss in manic activity.
Scrub, cook, pack, care for her family,
Attended the funeral, side by side with
Nana Pennifold, in turns silent or talking
non-stop about her lost daughter.
Everything of mother's was treasured,
lace collars, half-done knitting, hairbrush,
coral necklace and well-read books

A last departure from Horsted Keynes.
Nana and Rose waved through smoke clouds.
Emily wept, reluctant to leave her beloved home.
Freddie quiet, lulled by the rocking steam-puffer,
silent as they swept over the North Downs,
towards London and a strange unknown land.

3: A Family Torn in Half

Emily, my maternal grandmother came from Horsted Keynes in Sussex. Her parents were Betsey Pennifold, born in 1841 to a well-off farming family and William Field, a gamekeeper, married in 1861.

Betsey gave birth to 13 children between 1861 and 1881. Sadly, infant life was fragile in the nineteenth century. Thomas William Field, their second child born in 1862 died in 1865, and Florence Field died in 1877, only five years old.

Mystery surrounds the drastic removal of William Field and his family from Horsted Keynes in Sussex, to the banks of the River Stour in North Essex in 1881. *(see postscript 1)*

A family separated

Delving into the 1881 census pinpoints a tragic moment in my family story. Gamekeeper William had already moved to Wrabness in Essex, with his older children. However Betsey, heavily pregnant, had remained in Horsted Keynes, in Oddynes Cottage, where they had lived for twenty years, since their marriage. Betsey had newborn four day old twin boys on census night

Little Oddynes Cottage, Horsted Keynes 1881

Name	Relation	Age	Where Born
Betsey Field	Head-married	40	Cuckfield
Mary Anne Field	Daughter-unmarried	18 Servant	Horsted Keynes
George Edward Field	Son	3	Horsted Keynes
Frederick Harold Field	Son	4 days	Horsted Keynes
Alfred James Field	Son	4 days	Horsted Keynes

William was still working as a gamekeeper. I assume he had only just moved, and Betsey was expected to move soon after the birth with the other younger children to **Woodland, Wrabness, Essex.**

Name	Relation	Age	Where Born
William Field	Head- married gamekeeper	54	Sussex, Bolney
Ada Alice Field	Daughter- unmarried	17	Horsted Keynes
Annie Field	Daughter	14	Horsted Keynes
Arthur A. Field	Son Scholar.	7	Horsted Keynes
Betsey Field	Daughter	4	Horsted Keynes

Emily, 13, their other daughter, was living at School Cottage, Horsted Keynes, a "domestic nurse girl" for Alfred 3, and baby Frederick, the children of teacher Alfred Larter, 27, and his wife, Maria, 24. Betsey's new twins were also called Frederick and Alfred, a quad of Fred's! I feel that Emily would have been pulled between her employment and moving to Essex.

At this moment, their other son, Ernest 11, who had restricted growth, was staying at Dean House, Cuckfield, with his maternal grandparents, Eliza and Thomas Pennifold, a farmer of 175 acres.

Their oldest child, Eliza Jane Field, born 1861, was a pantry maid living at the Gilbridge Hotel, Eastbourne

Not only did the children have the ordeal of separation, but a month later, tragedy struck when Betsey died, and was buried in Horsted Keynes on May 18th, leaving her eleven children without their mother.

Little Oddyness Farm, Horsted Keynes

13

4: A Mistley Fairy Tale

Once there was, and once there was not
a mother who died at her twin boys' birth.
She whispered to her daughter and mother,
"A baby for each of you to care.
Feed them when hungry with love.
A shawl for each to keep them safe,
with blessings and to remember me."
Twins separated at the Christening,
before their mother's funeral.
In and out of time.

Little Emily cocooned her baby brother,
enveloped in his mother-knitted shawl,
both spell safe.
Journeyed on the smoke-whistler,
across a trickle river stuck in mud squelch,
to halt at Mistley, a malt-burning boat-loader,
a harbour of pollution and sewer disease.
Greeted by father resplendent
in gamekeeper's polished bowler hat.
He pushed the heavy hand cart
up the furrowed woodland track
In and out of time.

> *Footnote: from "Stour Secrets"*
> *Mistley could be named after mircel, an*
> *ancient name for the herb basil, combined*
> *with let, meaning pasture; or it may be*
> *named after a mistletoe wood.* K. Rickwood

Into the upside down world of Mistley Wood.
Roots sky climbed, fruits soil reclined.
William, silent, guided them toward Old Knobbly,

"Old Knobbly" in Mistley Woods

His tongue loosened, conjuring fear
"A 700 year old oak. Look out.
Beware hunted witches sheltered here,
as Matthew Hopkins hunted them down,
Twenty pounds for each conviction.
They do say..."
His daughter blanched.
A shadow shrouded the dapple tree light.
Emily clasped the baby tight.
Mother knitted shawl enveloped.
Both spell safe.
In and out of time.

A twig snapped, father sprang alert.
"A poacher, I'll catch the villain.
Keep to the path, up the hill,

15

to Keeper's cottage by Poacher's Pond."
Emily shivered in fear, baby whimpered.
She pushed the heavy hand cart
up the furrowed woodland track,
In and out of time.

At the path fork, Emily
followed the steep road less trodden.
By a bramble concealed cottage,
built on chicken legs and bones, sat
a tangled-haired, one-eyed crone,
sorting peas to eat from stone.
"Help me dear, I cannot see."
Witch-fearful, Emily stepped back,
and ditch-fell.
In and out of time.

Head bashed, spell-bound,
Emily stirred, no baby.
Head ache, cold damp compress.
A darkened smoke filled room.
Dried herb bundles, basil, rue, comfrey.
A cauldron roasting meat.
Emily leapt to her feet, alert.
"The witch will eat my brother."

A gentle lullaby, baby gurgle.
A chair rocking crone and bairn.
"Your mother blessed the shawl,
keeps you both safe."
Worries dispelled,
Emily cuddled her brother.
then, with thanks,
sorted peas from stone.
"Go safely on your path.
Circle turn, neither left or right."

16

Emily pushed the heavy hand cart,
up the furrowed woodland track,
In and out of time.

Home to the Gamekeepers cottage.
For ten long years, Emily, father and siblings
planted vegetables in their woodland clearing,
drank cool fresh spring water,
fished in Poachers' Pond, chopped log piles.
plucked chickens, pheasants and swan,
picked apples from mistletoe clumped branches.
Emily strolled over wood and marsh paths.
Herons glided, woodpeckers drilled,
poachers rabbited
and milliners feather gathered.
Emily circled, both left and right,
nowhere and everywhere, but found
no bramble cottage, no crone.
A lonely hidden stone doorstep still
stumble-trips blackberry gatherers,
In and out of time.

5: A new start in Mistley Wood

Life at Pond Cottage, Mistley

After the Field family move to the banks of the River Stour, Essex Petty sessions show that my great-great grandfather, William, continued to be diligent as a gamekeeper:

> *08.04.1882 summoned by William Field, gamekeeper to Mr. Travis Nunn, Wrabness, for unlawfully using snares, for the purpose of taking game, to wit hares.*

By 1888 William was gamekeeper at Mistley Hall:

> *28.03. 1888 summoned by William Field, gamekeeper to Mr. L. Kensit Norman J.P. for trespassing in search of rabbits on land in the occupation of Mr. W.T. Cook of Bradfield*

By the census of April 1891, Emily was housekeeper for her father, and caring for the younger children at

Pond Cottage, Mistley Hall

NAME	RELATION	AGE	WHERE BORN
William Field	Head Widower	Gamekeeper. 60	Sussex, Bolney
Emily Field	Daughter single	House Keeper 23	Horsted Keynes
Ernest W	Son single	Gardener. 21	Horsted Keynes
Austin Albert	Son single	Gardener. 17	Horsted Keynes
Betsy L	Daughter single	General Servant. 15	Horsted Keynes
George E	Son	Scholar. 13	Horsted Keynes
Frederick H	Son	Scholar 10	Horsted Keynes

Frederick's separated twin brother Alfred was raised by his uncle, farmer, Henry Pennifold and his wife Rose. By 1891, he was 10 years old, living with their four children, and his grandmother Emily, aged 72. Alfred lived his whole life in Sussex. The photo shows Frederick and Alfred (right) together as young men, but they grew up apart. Frederick lived with his father in Essex, before joining the Lancers in 1909.

Ernest, with restricted growth, is in the middle, infantilised by the photographer with a toy horse

After working as a gardener, Ernest later farmed turkeys almost his height. A circus tried to recruit him for high pay, but Ernest would not become a source of mockery. He stayed working on the land, until his death in 1918.

Of the other children, Mary Jane also moved to Wrabness to join her father, and in 1885 married a local agricultural worker, Joseph Rowland. In 1886, Annie Field married Robert Cullington, an agricultural labourer in Wrabness, and had 9 children. Ada married Robert Ollie a horseman from Great Oakleigh, Essex, in 1885, and had 7 children. The Field sisters continued to be very close and met regularly, throughout their lives. By the 1940s three sisters, 'Polly', 'Tot' and Ada lived in a cottage on Mistley Heath, with a large plum tree, and newspaper covering the table, which did not match Emily's (seated left in photo) high standards.

Eliza Jane, the oldest daughter 20, had left home before 1881 and was a pantry maid at the Gilbridge Hotel in Eastbourne. She remained living on the South Coast, moving to Bournemouth, after marrying Edward Towner a grocer. By 1911, her brother George had moved from Essex and was living with them, working as a hotel porter.

Emily Field, my maternal great-grandmother, married George Reason, maltster, soon after the 1891 census, in Mistley Church on 15th April. I imagine Betsy, her sister took over as housekeeper for their father and brothers. Emily quickly resumed her role as mother, as her first daughter Flo was born on 28th October 1891.

Church of St Mary and St. Michael, Mistley

6: Emily, the Gamekeeper's daughter in 1890

Deep in the midst of Mistley Woods,
in Pond Cottage, by Poachers's Pool,
in dappled shadows by daylight,
owl hoots echoing by moonlight,
remote from busy Mistley docks and Maltings,
lived Emily, the gamekeeper's daughter,
Housekeeper to her widowed father,
mother to her little sister and brothers,
Isolated in an ancient fairy tale cottage,
living out a story she never imagined.

Six days of hard work: a Cinderella.
Scrub floors, catch spiders and mice.
boil water, wash clothes, turn mangle.
Skin rabbits, pluck pheasants, feed hens.
Peel leeks, onions, potatoes, shell beans.
Bake bread, roll pastry, cook dinner.
Patch and mend, stitch and knit.
Evening eye strain to read by oil lamp.
Escape with Jane Eyre, Little Dorrit,
Wilkie Collins and Margaret Oliphant,
to adventure in unexplored worlds.

Relief on Sundays at Mistley Church.
dust dances in stained glass rainbows,
echoes of worship in Horsted Keynes.
Scent of beeswax candles and other people.
Sunday best, in home made skirts,
lace collared blouses, shining shoes.
William, her father, in bowler hat,
brothers in ties and Sunday best,
A pride of peacocks perching in the pew.
Emily listened intently to the lessons,
read with meaning by George Reason,

muscular, six foot tall, a joy to behold.
At service end, village girls crowded round,
George stood awkward, overwhelmed.
seemed unaware of Emily, gliding by.

Life turned inside out, one Mistley market day.
Emily bought sugar, cheese, flour, oysters.
A drunken coal-bargee Geordie staggered,
barged into Emily, liked what he saw.
Emily ignored him, walked quickly away.
Footsteps followed, she dodged round washing,
lines dancing merrily on Mistley Green.
Slipped up the side alley, past the graveyard,
heard beer-fuelled shouts, ran homeward.
Feared to look backward, shook in despair.
Ran into the tunnel under the railway,
hurtled into a massive giant, screamed.
"It's alright Emily, it's me, George Reason."
Screams and broken words echoed round,
at the tunnel end, a drunken shadow melted away.

Both clasped one another, as long as they could
Emily stared up into a concerned face, and
laughed with relief "A sailor followed me home."
"That scream would scare the hounds of hell away.
I'll walk you home, Emily." At last a chance!
The start of a fifty year journey together
through Easter, Whitsun, and Lammas
Harvest, Christmas and Candlemas,
a rhythmic spiral dance through time.

7: Firstborn riverside sister

Flo was born on the riverside, an old soul, swimming into a new life shouldering wisdom and common sense. Emily Reason, married for only six months, hoped the world would believe her baby was premature. Following their Christmas engagement, George had smuggled her into his lodgings at Cliff House in Mistley, after hearing their banns read for the first time. He had laughed about needing to warm her from the cold. Emily felt nervous "Should we be here?"

"Come on Em, we're almost wed. I can't wait forever." He lifted her high and swung her around in the air, then gently lowered her on the bed, and undid her buttons. Emily felt rushed as George kissed her too hard, his stubble grazing her cheek. He stroked her gently but then pushed hard against her womanhood. Squashed as he moved up and down, before he moaned, relaxed, grinned and kissed her. She felt overwhelmed and confused. "What if I get pregnant?"

"I'm your husband now, you'll always be loved."

But as George fell asleep, Emily felt shamed, dressed quickly and crept home.

George Reason outside the Maltings Foreman's Cottage about 1925

Emily ballooned in the last weeks of pregnancy, and knew the baby would take after George, tall and big boned, whereas Emily and her siblings were small. She worked out that nobody would be deceived, but with George's support knew their new family was important, not the local gossip. On their wedding-day, 15th April 1891, she walked as tall as possible for a small rounded woman.

Emily and George moved into the Foreman's Cottage, adjoining the busy Maltings on the Walls, Mistley. Early morning, trucks and workers' shouts replaced birdsong and wind rustling the trees at Gamekeeper's Cottage.

Giving birth was a struggle. Emily pushed and swore for 24 hours, transformed from a fairytale bride to a cawing cuckoo. A third low tide revealed the mud flats, but no baby emerged. Emily had feared childbirth. Her mother, Betsey, had died 10 years before, when the twins were born. Birth and death merged in her mind. She had been a good replacement mother at 13 for her brothers, baby Fred and little George. Now, she feared she was too small to give birth, and could only look after orphans, not be a real mother. As Emily's weary eyes closed, Betsey appeared by the bed, smiling, and holding out her hand. Emily longed to be safe in her mother's arms, again. Swans glided towards the sea with the departing tide, and Emily's soul soared. Polly her sister wiped her forehead with water "Em, you can't leave us now, keep trying. The midwife can see your baby's head. Stay with us, love." Determined to see this baby safely arrive, Em sat up, lowered her legs to the floor and tried to stand. Polly and Annie supported her under each arm, and with new found strength, Em started to walk, and gravity took over. She squatted by the window, and her baby pushed her way out. Polly leapt to catch her niece before she hit the floor. Long, firm and observant, Flo stared at her mother with profound eyes, and then gazed around. The river tide reversed and flowed back. The midwife shouted at her recalcitrant patient to return to bed for the afterbirth, but Emily although small was determined, and with all her strength, first cradled Flo to her breast, and then held her high to greet the returning swans soaring to greet their new neighbour.

After her birth on 28th October,1891, Flo dwelt on the riverside, her place in life for the next 82 years.

8: Bessie the invisible girl

Born 31st August 1894

George awoke, kicked in the back.
His unborn boy's feet and fists flailed,
in Emily's boisterous swollen womb.
He smiled at the prospect of a son,
to enjoy a first pint together,
to share skills, gardening, photography,
to help become a self-made man,
a strong young reflection of his father.

Emily's quick two hour labour ended,
George heard a robust male cry,
burst expectantly into the bedroom.
Smiling, Emily cradled her newborn.
His bubble burst, "Not another old girl."
Smile frozen, crestfallen, George bent,
kissed Emily perfunctorily on the forehead,
'At least you're both well and safe."
turned, downcast, descended,
to dig up fresh garden potatoes,
a more reliable crop

Emily worried at George's reaction,
not picking up his new daughter,
off to the pub straight from work,
disdainful at Bessie's christening,
distanced. Unconnected.

Bessie was a perfect child,
loving, smiling, gentle, helpful.
No trouble, but unnoticed by George,
although, Flo's constant companion.
Disappointed, George gave his firstborn
more encouragement and attention.
Both clambered on his knee for stories,

a giant reading to wide-eyed daughters.
Both inhaled his pipe tobacco
and his infectious laugh. But always,
George oblivious to Bessie's presence,
turned his gaze and words to Flo.

Desperate to please, Bessie strived,
but only became visible in disarray.
At two, making play biscuits from scraps,
Bessie was coated head to toe in flour dust,
George shattered Bessie's make-believe,
"It's uncooked. I can't eat raw pastry.
Emily, look at the mess she's made."
Bessie learnt to be a perfect cook,
became a model school pupil,
practical, industrious, studious.
Neat, clean, perfectly dressed,
tidy, never a hair out of place.
Nothing worked.
Bessie remained unnoticed.

Three years later, Millie's birth,
added to George's disappointment,
'Why does Emily only carry daughters?'
Dejected once more, "Not another old girl."
But Millie determined to stand out.
Loud, naughty, and outspoken
she gained her father's full attention.
If ignored, Millie clung around his knee
until lifted high and laughingly held.
George continued oblivious to Bessie,
walked right past the invisible girl,
so willing and eager to be held.

9: Millicent Dora

Millicent Dora was the central planet of her universe, where she expected family and friends to radiate around her sun. But they only ever called her Millie, and rarely fulfilled their purpose of making her the focus of their life. A disappointing crowd.

Millie was born on 25th July 1898, but was to belong firmly in the 20th century, a woman on her own terms. She announced her arrival with loud screams. Nobody could ignore Millie, she filled any room. Born with two adoring, maternal, older sisters, Millie gloried in her role as the youngest, smiling when her every need was met. Bessie brushed and plaited her wriggling hair, while Flo tied her escaping laces. But, when Millie turned 5, Ella and Elsie the twins were born. Millie's sweet smiles were replaced by grimaces, triggered by these two cuckoos in her nest. Bessie attempted to get her to brush her own hair, but she ended up in tangles, so she still got help. Millie did not hide her feelings, she stamped her feet, shouted, tossed her bunches, and ignored requests to lend a hand. "I'm reading my comic, I'm playing clock patience."

Then they tried to send her away to school. Bessie and Flo took one arm each and half carried Millie up the hill, and deposited her in the Infant class at the Methodist School. Millie made them late for the first time ever in the junior class. Millie stood up, and announced "I'm hungry and cold, I'm going home." Emily was not pleased to see her daughter return, and shocked Millie by shouting and dragging her back to be slapped by the teacher. Betrayal.

Millie spoke without considering her effect on others. Whilst kind to Ella, she constantly pointed out Elsie's cast in her eye, and pallid skin "My complexion is peaches and cream". Millie won friends with humour, a winning smile, and gossip. Followers brought her gifts to remain in her good books, but her moods could be destructive, reducing small girls to quivering heaps with comments on the wrong colour ribbons or snotty noses. Her mobile face was more changeable than a weather vane. She could be impressive, as she wrote funny rhymes in autograph books, joked and organised the playground leading skipping rhymes, not meant for adult ears. Whilst their mother's girls were always dressed practically in aprons, Emily's home-made lace collars were the envy of Manningtree. Millie flounced in her lacy glory, a princess among swine.

Millie had a sweet tooth. She was never satisfied, from infancy she chirped "I'm starving, I need more. I'm so hungry." Millie relished food, apart from potatoes; "Boring, too plain." Her prejudice continued into old age, how she hated peeling spuds. Baking with her mother was a delight, they laughed and chatted, considered recipes, in the warm kitchen hub. Her father even praised her "Pastry as light and tasty as your mother's." Millie was to become a cook in service like her two older sisters. Pleasure stemmed from counting stones in plum or cherry pies "Tinker, tailor, soldier, sailor. Rich man, poor man, beggar man, thief. Lady, baby, gypsy, queen." Millie had her life sorted "Queen. I'm going to be Cinderella, live in a palace and marry the prince." But her character was more suited to playing the ugly sister.

By 12, Millie was the oldest child at home, and no longer had to share a bed, after Bessie and Flo went into service, Millie ruled the roost and manipulated her two generous hearted twin sisters to fulfil all her desires. Elsie even brought her tea in bed every morning, until Emily had a strong word with her bossy daughter. Millie towered over her, but shrunk under her mother's quiet reprimand. However she then manipulated the twins into making her bed daily. Her short lived reign ended, when at 14, she became

Millie (L) holds Elsie, awkwardly, whilst Bessie appears relaxed holding Ella. Millie did not relish her role as big sister

a kitchen maid at Kingsford Park, the far side of Colchester. Homesick, she spent days scrubbing floors and cleaning pots and pans. Queen Millie was Cinderella again!

10: Elsie and Ella arrive in town

Buffalo Bill's brightly painted circus train roared past on the far side of the river, in the early morning of September 4th 1903. The Reason sisters jostled for position in the front room window on the opposite riverbank of the Stour. Millie shouted and imagined the inside of the distant wagons, "Look, cowboys on their horses, Red Indians, elephants, buffaloes. Best day ever and mum's finding another baby from the gooseberry bushes." Her older sisters smirked, with superior wisdom.

Flo scanned the brightly painted trucks excitedly, but her voice was commanding, a responsible big sister, wise for eleven, "Calm down Millie, you'll disturb mother. She's having the baby."

In her imagination, Bessie becomes Annie Oakley, the fast shooter, galloping beside the train. Aims her rifle across the river and shoots the pipe her dad is smoking as he paces back and forwards by the riverside. A sharp shooter. Her mother's scream destroyed her dream. The sisters grabbed each other for comfort. Flo tried to hide her feelings in work "I'll put the kettle on for tea." Bessie and Millie gazed longingly after the train of dreams, as it vanished towards Ipswich. Then slowly followed Flo into the kitchen. Flo confidently lowered the iron grate over the fire, and carefully put down the kettle, after filling it from the pump in the yard. Bessie peeled potatoes ready for dinner, and stringed beans with Flo, keen to be helpful, and to be praised by her father for once, while Millie carelessly played tiddlywinks into an egg-cup.

Upstairs, Emily was exhausted after hours of labour, 'this baby is too happy and settled in the womb.' She had never been so large or tired in pregnancy. Emily's waters had broken in the early hours. Her sisters, Polly and Ada, were supporting the local midwife, Susan; eighteen stone, red faced, glum, and pouring with sweat. Polly opened the window to clear away the goodwife's acrid stale smell. Emily, normally so calm and kind, exploded "Never again. Bloody George wanting a son. His fault all my babies are so big. This one is a giant. No easy birth." A sharp intake of breath, and a scream to crack the ceiling.

"I can see the head, a big push." A small girl slid out, reluctant to breathe, rubbed in a towel, Baby Elsie looked around lost, alone, and yelled for her other half, called her mirror twin. Emily started cramping painfully again "Something's wrong."

Susan peered through the mucus and blood, "Hold on. You're having another. We need a doctor."

"What? No I'm not, mother died having twins." Intense waves of pain crashed through Emily's body. After five minutes, the good wife had to slightly turn the baby, and shouted at Emily to keep pushing. Em felt her mother's hands pulling, offering relief from pain, but was kept earthbound by the plaintiff newborn miaow. She would not force Flo to become the twins' mother, or have her children separated like her twin brothers. Em breathed deeply in and out, and pushed. Ella appeared, still and blue. Another miniature doll child. She was not breathing.

Polly rushed down for hot water, and for seven minutes the doctor dipped Ella between hot and cold bowls of water, and slapped her back anxiously. Baby Elsie, cuddled in Aunt Annie's arms, watched wide eyed from her old wrinkled face. At last Ella took a sudden intake of breath, and whimpered. Ella looked for her twin, and both smiled. United again.

George arrived at Emily's bedside, anxious for his exhausted pale deflated wife. He kissed Em gently on her forehead, but blundered "What two more old gels?"

Emily roused herself and half sat up "You're lucky any of us are alive. We have five beautiful children, but there will be no more. If I'm dead, you won't manage, you'd be hopeless, lost"

George attempted to make amends "They are beautiful, like you, small and dark. A double gift."

Ever practical, Flo and Bessie cushioned the bottom drawer. and transformed it into a double cot, so the twins could be together. Knitted extra baby blankets, and smaller cardigans while Flo started a second rag rug. Flo mothered Ella, and Bessie mothered Elsie. Millie became the odd one out, 'piggy in the middle'. She dressed her china-head doll in her sisters' outgrown baby clothes, and talked non-stop to regain attention, previously enjoyed as the baby.

One rare photo of George, shows a giant smoking his pipe, and Emily, cradling one twin each. Normally he was photographer and developer, his photos proudly showing Emily with her girls. For once he has handed over his camera and holds Elsie at attention for the picture.

Elsie, Millie and Ella in wonderful home-made dresses about 1910

32

11: Flo goes into service

Flo was an old child for her age. She learnt quickly, was sensible and caring; a perfect older sister when Bessie was born. She taught Bessie to crawl, walk, talk, sew, read, write and add. Flo became less serious in the company of her playful, smiling sister, laughing together at this strange life. Millie arrived, made double the noise and had twice as many temper tantrums as her sensible older sisters

Once Flo's calm outer shell was shattered. Swimming proudly in the river at 7, the current started to drag her sea wards. Flo swam vainly against the tide, and had no voice to shout. George spotted his daughter's distress, and waded in fully clothed, in new foreman's outfit, and scooped her up. Flo cried hysterically as George carried her up the passageway, river mud dripping from his new boots. Flo was cradled in her mother's arms, for once a lost child.

Flo is on the left, in one of the first photos of all five sisters, about 1905. Flo is wearing adult style clothes, with a lace collar, made by their mother, Emily (left). Bessie, 11, and Millie 7, are wearing matching blouses. In front, Ella and Elsie also wear hand frilled dresses. Probably Emily involved her older daughters in making the clothes. Flo made her own outfits throughout life

Emily's older daughters loved helping their mother to cook, relishing her gentle guidance, scents of new bread baking, and the warmth of the range. All three became cooks in service. Flo was grounded in practicality, old beyond her years. Whilst Flo washed thoroughly, quickly pinned up her hair into a bun, echoed her mother's clothing, and looked 30 at 13; Bessie spent time looking in the mirror, choosing clothes, and brushing her hair 100 times until it shone. Millie used both sisters as lady's maids, delighting as they washed and dressed her, whilst she talked non-stop, delivering her commands. Flo rarely played, but devoured books, especially detective stories. Meanwhile, Bessie escaped into fairy-tales, and imaginary realms, rescued by handsome princes on white chargers. Millie loved dressing-up and parading in style, calling for constant praise

Flo, aged eleven and Bessie took over care of the twins, after their long tortuous birth, following which their mother had turned grey. Ella was permanently carried by Flo, and Elsie by Bessie. Millie resented losing her position as the baby, and never stopped talking in order to be noticed. Flo felt her duty to be the competent older sister, and projected an illusion of practised adulthood. Bessie was the only one who Flo trusted with her worries, although a temporary gap arose when Flo went to work at 13, whilst Bessie was still a tall, playful 10 year old.

At school, Flo was prepared for domestic service, in spite of being the brightest in the class. She was a girl! George borrowed the malting's cart to trundle her belongings across the river to Brantham Court, to start her post as a kitchen maid. Flo sent daily postcards planning her first Sunday off. After 4 hours work, cleaning out and lighting the fires, emptying the chamber pots, sweeping the stairs, Flo set off for home at last. Exhausted from her labours, Flo wanted to rush, but her legs were a lead weight. Grey river mists shrouded the day. The track split and, enclosed by high hedges, Flo had no idea which way to go. Wiping the corner of her eyes, she looked for a solution. Flo climbed a nearby stile, saw the right hand path led to the river road, jumped down and ran. She wanted her mum's Sunday roast. Then she froze as heavy boots approached. Out of the mist a grey giant appeared, Flo nearly turned and ran, then realised it was her dad. George cuddled her and noticed her tear smeared face, "It's a long way home by yourself." Arms round shoulders they plodded home for 3 miles, across the causeway, under the railway bridge, past the railway cottages, and hen sheds and along the High St, where Manningtree Church was turning out. The vicar ignored the riverside family, who chose to worship at Mistley Church. Flo savoured the smell of salt, fish and reeds as they turned onto the Walls. A rush of four white aprons enveloped Flo. Ella and Elsie pulled at their beloved sister's skirt. Emily dived down the path, wooden spoon dripping gravy still in her hand, and nearly knocked her tall daughter over with her embrace.

At half past three, the afternoon milk cart signalled time to return. Emily noticing Flo's black rimmed eyes, loaded her daughter with cake, cordial, and sewn rags, in case her monthlies started soon. Mother and daughter relished blackberries as they dawdled towards the station, unwilling to part. "Get back to Brantham quickly love, before the river mist descends." Flo bent down to kiss her mother goodbye. Emily watched her shrinking daughter retreat back to the reality of domestic service, and wept for her lost childhood.

Flo turned every few yards to wave to her mother, longing to run back home, but duty and pride won. At work nobody was sympathetic, because she looked older than her years. Flo was tall and well built. She was given no leeway, whereas Mary, who started work on the same day, was small, and treated gently. Mary shared an attic room with Flo, and cried every night. Normally Flo jollied her along, but that night she buried her head in the pillow to hide her tears. Flo felt alone for the first time ever, longing to return home to her family.

12: The chosen one

Hand crafted lace collar,
pinafores and schooldays discarded.
Loving care of small twin sisters,
unseen pinch to wriggling Millie,
family standards upheld.
Hair, dutifully brushed fifty times,
night and morn, dances sun gold.
Ambitious Bessie smiles,
glides Into the middle pews.
The foreman maltster's daughter,
gazes up at the hatted gentry.
Sunday scrubbed workers,
scrabble for space behind.
A disciple, anointed by Mrs. Norman,
virtuous vicar's wife,
to start a new life
as her kitchen maid.

Bradfield Rectory

Hard working Bessie,
eager to please, proud
to be "the chosen one."
Trunk packed; nightdresses,
Confirmation Bible, Sunday best,
monthly rags, rose water,
ebony brush embossed with a silver 'B'
stamps, stockings, stitching,
knitting, Woman's weekly, high
expectations and pride.
On previous rectory visits,
with her lay-reader father,
warmly welcomed at the front door,
by the towering genial rector,
a legend on the cricket field.
But the cart trots fast past
dreams of gracious life,
round to the back door,
Down the scullery steps,
a lowly servant descends
ambitious Bessie, just a kitchen maid.
Dreams shattered, Bessie
peels potatoes, polishes saucepans
scrubs sinks, washes floors.
'Best and cheapest?'
Bobby Best carbolic itches.
'One-O-One cleans
without scratching' but
blisters Bessie's red hands.
Sweat drips, hair straggles.
Whilst cook mixes Snow White
Whitworth's finest icing sugar,
butter, ground almonds, eggs,
and sweet raspberry jam.
She creates Maids of Honour,
whilst envious Bessie slaves,
only a lowly kitchen skivvy.

7). *Maids of Honour*

1/4 lb ground almonds, rather less than 1/4 lb moist sugar,
2oz. butter & 2 eggs.
Line some patty pans with puff pastry. Place a little raspberry jam in them, & cover this over with this mixture. Beat up the sugar & butter, add the almonds & lastly the eggs.
Cross each tin with fine strips of pastry & bake in a moderate oven.

Gracious Mrs. Norman floats
down the kitchen stairs,
to greet her 'chosen one.'
Bearing gifts; virgin aprons,
starched caps, hand cream,
plus an unused maroon
leather covered lined book,
sparkling fresh to record recipes.
Sweet scents stove waft.
"Cook, Bessie, gather here."
A cook's desk bears Mrs. Beaton
and Domestic Weekly magazines.
"Muriel is on loan from Mistley Hall
to encourage and teach you all.
Every night you will write and recall
all new recipes in your journal."
Ambitious Bessie smirks, selected,
anointed new cook-in-waiting.

13: Pineapple Pudding

Bessie stares at the high brick walls castling the kitchen garden. Imagination transports her to rescuing heroines imprisoned inside, perhaps another escaped nun from East Bergholt nunnery. Or maybe a Garden of Eden, snakes curling up apple trees, waiting to tempt her. Back in reality, her task is to meet the gardener, collect the seasonal fruit and vegetables on her morning list ready for today's menu. An arched gate guards the secret garden. Bessie clicks the latch, pushes sturdily forward, forehead now draped with a sticky spider web, dislodged by her entry. She brushes the cobweb away, stands and stares. Then steps over the threshold into wonderland. A robin sings a greeting.

The walled garden is even bigger than the cemetery. Peach, pear, plum and apple espaliers bow down, golden fruit laden. Onions sunbathe on freshly turned ground. Joseph , the chauffeur, cigarette hanging, oily haired, in shiny black, brass buttoned uniform, stands erect from leaning on the wall, and approaches with a swagger. Beware, a predatory wolf. "Hello, young Bess, come to learn a thing or two?" as he stands still in front of her, blocking the path Bessie blushes and hesitates, and remembers her playground strategies, 'don't show any fear.' "My name is Bessie, not Bess." She side steps Joseph, but leaves footprints on the hallowed soil.

Rescue. Jim, the gardener, in string tied trousers, white haired, ginger moustached, pipe in mouth, ruddy well-worn face and smiling, approaches. "Welcome Bessie. Morning Joseph, have you come to help with the digging? Be good to have a hand." Joseph slinks away, with a quick smirk back towards Bessie, who turns attentively towards Jim.

Jim proudly shows off his harvest to Bessie, wide-eyed at the variety. Not just cabbage, spinach and sprouts, but also broccoli, curly kale, and rainbow chard. A trellis of climbing beans in a geometric frame is echoed by a shadow triangle fence on the ground. Orange Turkish Squashes vie with American pumpkins, English marrows jostle with Italian zucchini, a forecast of wars to come. Jim describes his battles; early peas stolen by mice, pigeons pecking the sunflower seeds, and caterpillars destroying the lettuce, but he beat them all. His poison and guns massacred all invaders.

Bessie worries about the weird potatoes, some blue, some knob covered or misshapen. "Oh Mr. Jim, is it blight?"
Jim peers at his crop and roars with laughter "Young Bessie, you've got a lot to learn. Mrs. Norman likes to impress with new varieties of veg. She reads seed catalogues." He begins to show off his successes. Rows of purple, red and speckled beans, drying in the potting shed for salads and soups. Artichokes, asparagus beds, soldier straight rows of leeks, and celery in soot.

A hot manure aroma reeks from a long low brick and glass frame covered pit, proudly containing Jim's 28 pineapples. Bessie stares incredulous at her first sight of exotic fruit. Jim gives Bessie the chance to pick her first pineapple. She saws at the stone-like stalk and lifts the prickly overgrown 'pinecone'. Overwhelmed by pungent, metallic acidity, Bessie bursts out "How can anybody eat this hand grenade. It's been wallowing in sh-muck." Quickly she swallows her words, "Sorry Mr. Jim, I mean manure."
Jim's round stomach shakes with laughter. He welcomes this plain speaking young cook.
"Well I've never eaten one, so I don't know how they taste. They're not for the likes of us."

Back in the kitchen. Bessie, under cook's direction, removes the hard pineapple shell as well as some finger skin. Tasting a shaving, she savours the sweet acidity, and then soaks the pineapple in blood red Creme de Kir. She infuses a strip of lemon in milk over the fire, cuts pineapple rings and lines the mould, then mixes beaten eggs into the infusion. Cook teaches her the new word 'garnish' as she decorates the pudding with pistachios, strange unknown nuts, delivered from Fortnum and Masons, not available in the local shops. An intoxicating concoction, Bessie relishes a small left over slice. Cook says the best way to cook is to taste all the time. Her size bears truth to her maxim. Bessie writes the recipe of new delights enthusiastically, and sends postcards to Flo and mother about this strange new fruit. Then with Mrs. Norman's blessing, Bessie takes a left-over slice to Jim, for his first taste of his perfectly grown pineapples. Jim is grateful for Bessie's kindness, but unimpressed "A bit strange. Not like good apple pie with custard."

Pineapple Pudding

Bessie's Recipe number 9

Put 1/2 pint new milk into a stewpan with a strip of lemon rind & infuse for 20 mins.

Mix a 1/4 lb. butter, 1/4 lb. caster sugar 1/4 lb .flour &1 1/2 oz. Creme de Kir, add the prepared milk.

Stir over the fire till it boils, turn it into a basin to cool then mix in 3 yolks of eggs & three whites stiffly beaten & 2 tablespoons diced pineapple.

Have ready a plain mould well buttered & decorate with pineapple cut in rounds.

Put mixture into the mould & steam 1 hour.

Garnish the dish with pineapple & pistachio nuts.

Serve with wine sauce or a sweet sauce

14: Lobster Soufflé a la Cannes

Woken at dawn, by the cock's crow
Bessie, kitchen under-cook, rises,
relishes indoor toilet warmth, and dresses.
Lonely, misses Millie's morning chatter,
brushes hair, glances in the mirror
and descends to daily drudgery.

Quick cuppa.
Clean out the kitchen range,
shovel hot coals to outside cinder heap,
dampen last ashes with used tea leaves,
to restrict clouds of coal-dust.
Sweep out and sneeze.
Scour off grease.
Blacken the cast iron,
retrieve hot coals.
At last, relight the stove.

Polish and spit.
Cook comes to inspect.
Hair pulled back, sculptured scowl,
Muriel sniffs, fingers a missed crack.
Hawk eyes scan, stare in triumphant disdain.
"Could do better, even soot on your nose."
Bessie upset, wipes away black tears.
"Scour the sink.
Scrub the floor.
Gather the eggs.
Then, make breakfast."

Mid-morning kitchen sparkle.
Muriel marches back, with fish-market trawl.
Bangs down a wriggling wet paper pile.
"Lobster, fresh caught and barnacle free.

You must learn proper French cookery,
Lobster Soufflé a la Cannes for lunch.
Boil water.
Get nutcrackers and skewers."
Unwrapped, the lobster fights her last battle,
claws desperately, pincers snap. "Careful.
Hold firmly across her back. Drop in the pan.
Mind, she'll break your fingers in two."
Lobster rises in a desperate death-throw,
clatters the lid.
Drowning, waves farewell.
Bessie the murderer, shares her terror.

Drained lobster, dressed now in blood-red shell.
"First separate the claws.
Pull off thumbs.
Break with nutcracker.
Throw away cartilage.
You don't want to choke the Mistress.
Crush the claws."
Post-mortem torture!
"Remove spines from back, shell crack.
Scoop out meat.
Peel tail.
Pick out sand-track.
Add green liver and fat to my fish-stock."
Bessie glares at the sparse edible pile,
result of cruel butchery and murder.
Sweeney Todd would gather more flesh.

Soufflé preparation requires more toil.

Bessie's Recipe 22:
Lobster Soufflé a la Cannes

Finely chop lobster,
Add purée of boned anchovies
Red Carmine essence, and a gill of cream,
Rub pulp of four tomatoes through wire sieve.
Stir on fire till warm, Remove from heat.
Mix in raw yolks. Stir in stiffly beaten white of eggs.
Put mixture in a buttered soufflé dish.
Surround with a frill of buttered paper
Sprinkle browned bread crumbs on top.
Add a small piece of butter here and there
Sprinkle on shaved truffle.
Bake to a pretty fawn colour.

Mrs. Kensit-Norman, the rector's wife, appears,
rounder every day. Suddenly retches
as she smells stale seashells: then
spots Bessie's tear-stained cheeks.
Breathes in deeply, then regains quiet control.
"Lobster soufflé is too rich for me at present
Bessie please cook me simple scrambled egg.
Muriel, I am aware you are teaching culinary skills.
but this is Wednesday lunch in a country vicarage.
Not Mistley Hall, entertaining dinner guests."
Muriel sniffs, bangs down the hot papered dish.
Shocked, the soulful soufflé sinks and shrinks.
Copying out the recipe, silently Bessie smiles.

15: Puree of carrots

Bessie's Recipe 28

*Take 1lb of carrots. Put them in cold
water with a little salt and bring to the boil.
Strain & rinse then put into the stew pan with
enough light stock to cover. Add a little liquid
Carmine & Apricot Yellow & a dust of castor sugar.
Simmer the carrots til tender then strain them &
press dry & pound them into a paste with 3 plainly
boiled potatoes & rub the purée through a hair sieve
Add a piece of butter & a little cream & stir til
boiling and use.*

Bessie washed fresh garden veg,
bottle green spinach, snug broad beans,
purple sprouting broccoli, rusty shallots,
feathery topped carrots from military rows,
marmalade orange and butter cream shaded,
fresh scented, long rooted from sandy soil.
Muriel's eyes gloomed, lips pursed, scowled.
She slammed down the basket, furiously,
"I want all orange carrots not pale parsnips."
Gardener Jim winked at young Bessie.
"Them all carrots. Wrong season for 'nips.
Them or nothing, your choice, Mrs. Cook."
Muriel glared "My carrot purée will be orange.
Watch and learn from the best, Bessie."

No watching for Bessie, as usual she slaved.
"Add colouring, Carmine (crushed beetles)
and Apricot Yellow (livid with lurid toxic paint).
Simmer, strain. Pound into a smooth paste
with three mashed potatoes. Rub into a purée

through a wire sieve. Add butter and cream."
Bessie mashed reluctantly, aware of lost
mouth-watering fresh carrot taste,
replaced by sticky fake orange paste.

Muriel proudly served Lamb Fillets a Montrose
smothered in Devil's Paste of mustard and chutney,
nested on Puréed Carrots, forced through a rose pipe,
and garnished with Kidnapped Kidneys.
Reverend and Mrs. Kensit Norman grimaced
over cold florid sweet orange carrot purée,
prickled at Devil's Paste (in a Godly rectory!)
scraped their ornamental meal to one side.

Mrs. Kensit-Norman, inspected Bessie's recipe book,
every detail laboriously recorded over two pages.
Mangled recipes to torture good food.
"Bessie, what special recipes you have learnt.
Now, you need to widen your experience.
You will spend a month learning from Rose,
my aunt's good plain cook, at Elm Lodge.
Bessie will be cook when she returns
and Muriel you will go back to the Hall,
where you shine at complex culinary display."
Both Bessie and Muriel smiled in delight:
escape from an unhappy partnership.

Wrapped in love, Bessie relaxed,
home for Sunday lunch, tucked into
roast potatoes, juicy lamb, mint sauce,
suet pudding, carrot mash, pale and sweet.
Millie hair tossed "No potatoes or carrots.
Them's dirty from the muck." Father barked
"Quiet. All joints on the table to be carved."

Millie flounced, slowly lowered her elbows.
Emily, Millie and the twins poured intently over
Bessie's recipe book. Emily, unimpressed by
unnecessary fuss, sighed at Bessie's distress.
"You'll be much happier cooking at Elm Lodge."

16: Bessie's Recipes from Elm Lodge

47 Rice Cake
6oz butter. 1/2 lb of sugar, 1/4 lb of flour
4 eggs (whites beaten to stiff froth)
Beat butter and sugar to a cream, add the rice & flour
then the white of eggs & stir till it looks white
then add yolks. Bake 1 hour

56 Scotch Shortbread
3/4 lb flour, 1/4 lb ground rice 1/2 lb good fresh butter 1/4 lb castor
sugar. Mix all well together with the hand
until stiff enough to roll out in finger lengths or with a cutter.
A yolk of egg is an improvement to the colour. Bake in a slow oven

After lunch, George drove Béssie to Elm Lodge.
She shivered as they skirted the cold Workhouse,
full of tramps, abandoned babes, and lunatics.
Ominous dark shadows crossed their future paths.
Down a sun splashed bluebell lane to Elm Lodge,
ivy covered, with precise box-hedged flower beds.
Bessie was welcomed with chatter and good cheer,
by Rose, plump with scrubbed red cheeks,
smile broader than the River Stour at high tide,
hair of ginger and grey tabby wayward curls.

Rose looked up at Bessie, hair shining and neat,
only fourteen but tall, with a gentle smile.
Over a cup of tea, Rose chattered non-stop
told her story with no emotion or frills.
An orphan raised in the workhouse,
rescued by Miss Norman at twelve,
A kitchen maid, then cook in charge.
Bill the baker proposed 20 years ago.
Every Sunday they walked out, whilst
Bill waited for Rose to reply. But fragile
Rose felt safe in her Elm Lodge kitchen.

"I'd love to learn you cookery
I learnt to read and write recipes, and
done numbers at our Sunday School.
Learnt to cook in workhouse kitchen.
Bet you know a lot from your mother."
Bessie smiled, felt at home with Rose.
"Miss Norman has such a sweet tooth.
Mainly I bake cakes, and tasty snacks."

Silver haired, wafer-thin, sparrow alert,
Miss Norman peered over half glasses,
ceased stitching her tapestry, inspected Bessie.
"I hear you're hard-working, diligent and clean.
I hope you don't waste time preening."
Bessie squeezed into the cluttered room,
poodles sniffed, chairs horse-hair stuffed.
cross-stitched covers and antimacassars,
Miss Norman peered at Bessie up and down.
"You'll do. Dear Rose will teach you to cook.
My tastes are simple, good afternoon tea,
medicinal brandy, cheese straws and egg-nog,
small cakes, sweet pastries and puddings.
No tough meat or fancy French recipes.
Ignore what you learnt from sour Muriel."

Bessie relished the new kitchen regime,
varied new recipes, written at speed.
Lemon Jelly (thick), Orange Marmalade,
to accompany Baking Powder Scones.
Ginger Cake, Plum Pudding, Mincemeat,
Sardines a la Croute, Liver Savoury

> *Cook pheasant or chicken livers,*
> *pound and season.*
> *Put in a slice of bacon,*
> *And cook for five minutes.*
> *Serve on croute.*

Geneva Pudding, Marble Cake, Eclairs,
Easter biscuits and Chocolate Pudding.
Bessie enjoyed sharing recipes from home,
Rice cakes, Marmalade Pudding, Ginger nuts,
and Barley water for Miss Norman's acid-reflux.

After Whitsun, relaxed and confident,
Bessie returned to Bradfield Rectory,
to a happy kitchen, without Muriel.
But disapproval arose from Mrs. Norman
"My aunt was pleased with your meals,
but your recipe book is slapdash.
Look at 92, Soup. What sort?

> *Stock thickened with cornflour*
> *& a little cream*
> *pieces of macaroni put in*
> *Serve with Parmesan*

Others should be able to follow it.
Even lazier is 94 Sandwich Cake

> *1/4 each of flour, butter, sugar.*
> *a little salt & bp. Mix as usual*

I expect better from my cook."

50

Every new recipe was diligently written,
carefully overseen by Mrs. Norman, who
weekly checked and planned her meals.
Encouraged Bessie to try new recipes:
102 Salted Almond Soup, Roman Pie
Floating Islands and Turkish Delight.
She Included varied ingredients, truffles,
anchovies, turbot, and dried apricots
Bessie recorded all methods in detail
eager to regain Mrs. Norman's approval.

Bessie wrote weekly to friendly Rose,
missed her warm support and laughter,
swopped recipes, gossip, jokes and news.
After Miss Norman passed away, aged 90,
Bessie was bridesmaid for Rose and Bill,
twenty years after his first proposal.

Bessie's recipe book changes totally after the tortuous recipe for Purée of Carrots.

*Recipe 29 Lemon Jelly (thick) is on a new page with Elm Lodge written next to the title.
All the following pages until Recipe 97 are headed Elm Lodge or EL.*

*Recipes are simpler, mainly for cakes and puddings, with main courses such as
Stewed Pigeons, Fish Dish, Croute and Po Soup!*

29   Lemon Jelly (Sheila)   Ethel Seelye

Put into 1/2 pt boiling water the rind of 1 1/2 lemons
peeled very thin & simmer 1/4 hour then add 6 oz loaf
sugar let it all dissolve then stir it into 3 well
beaten eggs with the lemon juice stir it on the fire
till it thickens have ready 1/4 g gelatine dissolved
in 2 table spoonfuls of water mix all ~~wel~~ well
together & put into a mould

____

30   Orange Marmalade
21 Seville Oranges. 4 lemons cut up very fine.
To every pound of bulk, 2 pints of cold water.
Soak for 24 hours. boil bulk till tender without sugar
when cold add 1 1/4 lbs sugar to every pound of fruit
& boil to a good jelly

31   Baking Powder Scones
1 1/2 lb of flour 1 1/2 oz lard 3 tea spoons baking powder
Sufficient milk to make a paste. Cook in a hot oven without delay

____

52

32   Ginger Cake

1 1/2 breakfast cups of treacle, 2 of flour, 1 teaspoon
cinnamon, 1 large dessertspoon ginger, 1 egg, 1/2 teaspoon carb
soda, 1/2 cup milk & lard or butter mix all the dry
ingredients, warm the treacle, put it into with the melted
fat, beat the eggs, dissolve the soda in the milk which
should be warm, beat all well together & bake in a slow oven

_____

33   Plum Pudding   (Elm Lodge)

1 lb breadcrumbs, suet, raisins, currants & candied peel
3/4 lb sugar 1 nutmeg & a little salt.
Beat 8 eggs add a wine glass of brandy a little browning.
Boil 12 hours. 3 times this quantity makes 5 good puddings

_____

34   Mincemeat

1/2 lb suet, 1 lb stoned raisins, 1 lb minced apples, 1 1/4 lb currants
1 1/4 lb raw sugar, 6 oz candied peel, 1 large lemon boiled, rind
of one grated, 1/4 teaspoon mace & ginger, 1/2 gill sherry, 1/4 g nutmeg
1/2 gill brandy a tumbler full in all

35   Potato Cakes   E. S

2 oz butter 2 g sugar 2 1/2 g potato flour 1 eggs a little b. p.
Mix as usual & bake in a hot oven

44   Marble Cake   Elm Lodge

Same ingredients as Genoise Pastry but mixed same as
Sandwich Cake, colour 1 part with chocolate 1 with cochineal
+ 1 part as it is. Bake & ice with water icing pink & white
+ using 1/4 lb icing sugar

45   Sponge Sandwich   Elm Lodge

2 eggs 4 tablespoons each of castor sugar & flour.
Beat eggs & sugar 10 minutes add flour & a little
b.p. Bake in a moderate oven 10 minutes

46   Plum Cake   E. L.

6 oz each of butter & sugar beaten to a cream add 5 eggs
& 9 1/2 oz flour then 4 oz each of currants & sultanas +
a little chopped peel. Bake 2 hours

47   Rice Cake

6 oz butter, 1/2 lb sugar, 1/4 lb ground rice, 1/4 lb flour
4 eggs beaten to stiff froth.
Beat butter & sugar to a cream add the rice & flour
then the whites of eggs stir till it looks white
then add yolks Bake 1 hour

Research on Elm Lodge and Bradfield Rectory

In searching the census around Bradfield I was unable to find where Elm Lodge was situated or who lived there. The recipes suggest an elderly lady with a sweet tooth. I am unsure how long Bessie spent at Elm Lodge. Clues from seasonal ingredients are absent. Did Bessie just copy or make all the recipes? I imagined Rose and Miss Norman, but they became alive for me, as I wrote.

Cooks needed a basic education to record recipes. Most schools trained girls for service, with a cookery syllabus. At the Wesleyan School in Manningtree, the older girls went once a week to the Public Hall, which only had one oven. They cooked or cleaned on alternate weeks. Many workhouse girls ended up in service. Often as exploited, underpaid skivvies.

After Bessie's return to Bradfield Rectory, her recipes are fuller and more varied. Recipes no longer rely on French titles, apart from soufflés.

In the 1911 census, for **Bradfield Rectory***, Bessie is the kitchen maid in a household with six servants. She is the only person allocated to the kitchen, so I assume she had a lot of responsibility for a 16 year old. Questions spring to mind? How did they relate to each other? Did Bessie cook for them all?*

NAME	RELATION	AGE		BORN
Thomas Kensit Norman	Head	48.	Clergyman	Portishead
Mary Constance Norman	Wife	34		Padbury Bucks
Thomas Kensit Norman	Son	1		Bradfield
Phyllis May Norman	Daughter	3		Bradfield
Beneford Ellis Lovett	Servant	26	Parlourmaid	Debenham Suffolk
Laura South	Servant	15	Nursermaid	Rivenhall, Essex
Bessie Reason	Servant	16.	Kitchenmaid	Mistley, Essex
Elizabeth Sarah Creek	Servant	27.	Housemaid	East Hanningfield
Rose Almond	Servant	29.	Nurse	White Waltham, Beds
Joseph William Liggins	Servant	27.	Coachman Chauffeur	Leicester

Joseph, the chauffeur, lived in separate quarters away from the female servants in the main household. His parents were local publicans. Apart from Bessie, none of the other servants were local, they may have moved to Bradfield, with the Kensit-Norman family, when the rector took over his father's living.

17: The first war casualty

Early evening light threw welcome shadows after a scorching day in August 1914. Wasps buzzed, threatening, as the twins, Elsie and Ella, jostled to gather windfall plums. One hungry wasp whined and darted at the plum thieves. Elsie shrieked, dropped her basket of now twice bruised fruit, and sheltered behind Ella. "Don't worry Elsie, the wasp wants to eat the plums not you, they're sweeter. We need Flo, she'd squash them all, with her bare fingers." Elsie's face shrivelled with thrill and horror.

While their older sisters, Flo, Bessie and Millie were all cooks in service, the joyful pair were still at school, not learning much. They mainly taught the infants to read, write, scrim by shredding cloth to stuff cushions, knit and sew, and collect and label flotsam for the nature table. Only the boys, 11 years and older, learnt algebra, science, geography and history. The girls were just taught domestic skills ready to go into service. Society had low aspirations for women in 1914. At the start of the war, their dad pointed out the boys needed geography to know where they would be sent to fight.

Their oldest sister, Flo, had given them stamps from India, where her fiancée Neville Sage's regiment, 4th Worcester Battalion, had been posted in 1911. The twins had teased Flo, when she first walked out with Nev after church parade, in full military red bandsman regalia "You've got scarlet fever. You love a soldier."

Emily darned George's thick brown socks. George would soon be home for supper after his early evening beer, to get the grain dust out of his throat. Emily teased him that tea would be just as good at quenching his thirst. Yesterday they had laughed over the phoney war, everyone on high alert over nothing, jumping

at their own shadows. The military guarding the railway viaduct had spotted possible invaders and fired their rifles at the imaginary foe, causing alarm on both river banks. Pompous Police Inspector Howlett from Mistley hearing a dozen rifle shots, rushed to investigate. But a cat darted in front of his bicycle, he fell heavily and was carried semi-conscious, bruised and black-eyed into the Skinners Arms, where it took three brandies and a pint for him to revive. George roared with laughter "Our first war casualty."
(Details from Essex Chronicle August 1914)

As the latch clicked, Ella and Elsie dashed to the back-gate to be the first swung up high in the air by their father. George pushed the gate slowly, brushed his girls aside, walked heavily into the kitchen, and silently dropped into his chair. As Em went to pull off his boots, she saw a tear flow into his moustache. George never cried. "It's started, the first casualty list is up, Nev's brother Arthur died in Flanders on August 26th. War's not a month old and young men already slaughtered." Elsie and Ella froze hand in hand. Both were in love with Arthur, only just twenty, with thick black hair and dark eyebrows, they had argued over which sister he would marry at the war's end. They had imagined a double wedding of brothers and sisters with Flo and Nev. Dreams shattered.

Emily reacted practically to the emergency: "We must telegram Flo, she won't have heard in London. Nev might not hear for a while, he's on a ship to the Balkans. No way she can comfort her fiancée. We must pay our respects to Mr. and Mrs. Sage."

George tried to reassure Emily: "Thank God we have girls. They won't die on the battlefield. They'll outlive this bloody war." The first time ever he seemed happy to have no sons.
A shiver ran down Emily's spine. A buried whisper "Someone just walked over my grave. Don't tempt fate, George." Emily pulled her girls towards her, and squeezed her precious twins. "I want to keep you safe at home forever. I don't want you to ever grow up."

Be careful what you wish for, it may come true!

18: Green Tomato Pickle Triptych

Bessie's cookbook 147 Green Tomato Pickle

*5lbs green tomatoes, 1/2 lb onions, 1/2oz ginger, 1/2lb sugar
1/2oz cloves, 1/2 oz. peppercorns, 1/2 oz. long peppers or a few
chillies,1/2oz mustard seeds, 2 pints vinegar. Slice
tomatoes and salt and let lay 12 hours. Slice the
onions, bruise ginger, grind cloves and peppercorns.
Drain tomatoes and boil all together.*

1915
Enter Bradfield rectory kitchen garden.
Tomato plants wander, unstaked,
thick leaves, tangled trusses,
while gardeners dig trenches in Picardy
not for crops, only for corpses
in war's tired tilled soil.

Practical Bessie, kitchen maid,
pushes back trusses,
hunts green tomatoes.
'Waste not, want not.'
Spiders scatter surprised,
to secret, silver dew-drop webs.
Bessie, sleeves rolled up, strong, smiles.
Satisfied,
harvests two baskets of hard green fruit,
and leaves her secret walled garden.

Pick, chop, salt, pickle.
Boiling vinegar, and oriental spices
tickle the vicar's wife's delicate nose
'Atishoo, atishoo, we all fall down.'

Jump forward to 1955

Pick, chop, salt, pickle.
Sheila, Bessie's granddaughter
pushes the latch, pantry creeps.
A seven year old hunter gatherer.
Eagle eyes, lips licked.
Dessert spoon ready, eager
Sheila surveys the shelf:
tinned spaghetti hoops,
baked beans, and peas.
Bird's custard powder,
marmalade with golly labels.
Packets of Angel Delight,
vegetable rack of giant marrows,
papery onions, dirty carrots.
Pale green utility cups hung on hooks.

Pick, chop, salt, pickle
I spy three full jars of
Great Auntie Flo's best ever
green tomato chutney.
Another jar open, half eaten.
Lid struggle, spoon dip.
Scent of lemon, sugar, spice.

Just one more mouthful.
No one will ever know.
"What are you doing now?
You can't eat chutney on its own."
Joan, Sheila's mother,
Bessie's daughter, shouts.
Sweet bitter pickle taste
triumphs over one smacked thigh.
Victory.

Sheila cooks Green Tomato Pickle in 1997

Pick, chop, salt, pickle.
Show courage,
beat cancer, keep busy.
I visualise; waves to extract poison ivy
and swirl with seaweed in ocean currents.
Right side mastectomy healing,
temporary cotton wool boob,
soft against the weeping scar.
First chemotherapy session yesterday,
slept all day, awake all night.

Cancer remedy for negativity:
cook green tomato chutney,
memories of childhood comfort.
Sick body rejects the stink.
Hot vinegar invades my nose.
Green chlorophyll chokes,
Stomach heaves, nauseous.
Red faced, blotchy, I cry.
Garden escape, kick a tomato truss.
Mourn Joan my mother.
Glad she is not here to fuss,
long for her warmth.
Sleep, supported by memory:
rest is best on a garden bench.

Dorian takes over husbandry.
Sterilises bottles. Green
tomato pickle potted
Six months later, I try
to taste the chutney.
Stench of boiled cabbage,
of dead green chlorophyll
Poison creeps from the opening lid.
Jars hidden in the old gas meter

cupboard, lost for ten years.
Then dustbin tipped,
jars not washed, not recycled.
Green tomato pickle wasted,
not wanted, not eaten.
Just memories remain.

Cancer impacts families.
Resting with Jenny, who at sixteen became the 'perfect'
teenager. When she started answering me back again, I knew I was
better.

Dorian passed his ten-year probationary period after giving amazing
support in crisis. Tea and sympathy led to a wedding

19: Roman pie 1916

Roman Pie

*Make a good white sauce, and add
the following- the remains of a cold
chicken or any white meat, cut in thin
slices, 2oz macaroni (boiled till very tender)
2oz grated cheese, pepper and salt and a
little cream. Line a soufflé dish round the
sides with short pastry, fill up with the
mixture and bake for about an hour.
Serve in dish that it is cooked in.*

Bessie finished adding a gathered hem to Patricia's little blue checked dress. "Well done Bessie. Make do and mend. Our bit for the war effort." Mrs. Norman smiled complacently.

Bessie hid her scowl. Her family had always reused every scrap: clothes were handed down, and eventually used for rag rugs. War was meant to be an effort by everyone, but the gentry still stole the cream of the milk. Mother struggled to buy flour, queued for two hours at the general stores for butter or greasy margarine, and again at the butchers for scraggy off cuts. Whilst in Bradfield, the rectory grocery order was nearly always complete. Although tasteless beet sugar had replaced cane. The rector might be mighty in Mistley, but even he could not stop the shelling of food convoys at sea!

Bessie spent two hours preparing ginger cake and cheese straws for Mrs. Norman's Thursday afternoon 'Knitting socks for soldiers' club. Posh ladies could embroider, but struggled to grasp the difference between knit and purl. Whilst Bessie served tea, she longed to grab the needles, pick up dropped stitches, and teach the basics. She reckoned '*The twins could knit better in the Infant class. In the same time a dozen ladies natter and knit just a few rows, I'd finish a pair of socks. I'm wasting time. I could do much more for the war effort.*'

Wounded local lads returned on crutches from the trenches, unable to fight again. Every Sunday, Reverend Norman listed the dead. Then Bessie listened to patriotic sermons, encouraging men to leave their reserved work in the Maltings and join-up. Bessie knew a Woman's Army was being formed as well, to release more men for front line duties. Without women joining up, the war could last forever.

Bessie went home on the next Sunday afternoon off. The house was so quiet and subdued since Ella became so ill with TB of the spine. Everyone tiptoed around to avoid disturbing Ella. Laughter was subdued in their once lively home. Bessie talked to mother about enlisting, as they pushed Ella in her wheelchair along the Walls to gather young nettles for soup. Mother only half heard, she was tucking Ella up with an extra blanket. Ella, so thin, coughing and shivering, even on a sunny spring day. "You know your father's views on women in trousers."
'I'm 21 years old. I'll decide. Besides Father always wanted me to be a boy. His wishes will be granted." Emily shook her head at her normally compliant daughter's heated reply.
Ella whispered "Bessie you're so brave. You would make lovely food for the troops. But we'll miss you. All our big sisters will have moved away."
"Ella, I'll come home on leave. We'll all be together for Flo and Nev's wedding"
Ella smiled, distracted by a hissing swan guarding her eggs on the river bank. Mother hoped Ella would live long enough to see the young cygnets fly their nest, like her fledgling daughters. She wanted to keep her girls safe at home forever, but also witness their onward flight into womanhood. But not too far away.

On Monday, Mrs. Norman waved a magazine recipe for Roman Pie in front of Bessie. "This is economical and will also use up the leftovers."
Bessie stopped herself from saying "When have I ever wasted any food?"
The recipe was a rich woman's idea of frugality. Bessie enjoyed making a new dish, but inwardly questioned the number of ingredients. 'Both pastry and macaroni? Plus precious cheese as well as half a chicken, and even added cream. Enough ingredients for a couple of meals. Roman Pie will make no difference to the war effort'.

The rector's family relished the crusty pastry and creamy chicken. Bessie and the two remaining general maids, not yet tempted by high factory wages, had poor-woman's Roman Pie. Bessie scraped off scraps of thigh, legs and belly, before she put the bones into the stock pot. She added parsley to the white sauce for extra taste to make up for no cheese or cream. 'One rule for the rich and another for the poor.' That evening, Bessie secretly completed a form to enlist for the Woman's Army. Then wrote up recipe 111 for Roman Pie.

Roman leftovers pie 2020

Forty days into Covid 19 quarantine,
I wake exhausted from intense dreams,
Coronavirus lockdown explodes emotions.
Four years today since my spinal-op,
rescued from encroaching paralysis by
six NHS surgeons in a six hour operation.
Now my altered life is lockdown confined.
Exercise on walking frame, round the block.
abandoned dog-turds rot, pigeons mock.
Lilac blossom snows, passers-by dodge.
Avoid wheezes and sneezes. Isolate.
Keep your distance. Stay safe at home.

Back to 1916, to Bessie's recipe book.
Connect by baking wartime Roman Pie,
less risky than Ouija board's spry spirits.
I play at cookery, while my husband slaves.
Buys ready-made super-market pastry,
(still available, as hoarders fight over flour)
prepares cheese sauce, without lumps,
scrapes chicken scraps off the carcass.
Cupboard hunts our hidden soufflé dish,
a marbled brown Poole pottery 80s gift,
from my mum, Joan, a generational link.
I add abandoned veg, on their last legs:

lonely leek, gritty from the farm shop,
one bolted onion, peel, chop and sauté.
Thinly slice a solitary, lost courgette,
grill five slices of last-day streaky bacon.
Grate double the cheese, find Creme-fraiche,
lurking soulful at the back of the fridge.
Add to sauce for complex 2020 taste!
Bessie shakes her head at the mix-up.
I line the dish with shortcrust pastry.
Criss-cross leftover strips on top.
Bake for 45 minutes at Gas Mark 6.
Success, crisp pastry and a rich taste.
Next day, even better cold than hot.
Comforted by a hundred year old meal
as Bessie and my mum nod in approval

20: Boiled sweets

Elsie ran downhill from school, stopped at the corner shop and bought a farthing worth of boiled sweets to cheer up Ella. That morning her twin had a head ache, and complained about the sunlight, so mother had closed their pink flowered curtains to protect Ella's eyes. Elsie skipped up the passage and froze at the kitchen door. Ella's wheelchair stood empty by the table, Ella's jigsaw still only half completed, but pieces were scattered on the floor. Ella and their mother had vanished. Elsie panicked, "Where are you?"

Elsie followed a hushed murmur down the darkened hall. She felt suffocated by the pungent aroma of frantic cleaning, overshadowed by the cloying scent of sickness. A white sheet soaked in disinfect, a last attempt to kill the germs, was nailed across the front sitting room door. Her mother pushed past the sheet, hugged Elsie close, and whispered "Ella's very ill. It's meningitis." Tears choked back, "Don't go in, you might catch it as well." Elsie rubbed her eyes, and called out to her twin "Ella, I'm here. I love you so much."
Ella through her swollen dry throat, whispered "Elsie, me too."

One of the last photos of Ella, before she was unwell
Back row from left: Bessie, Millie and Emily. In front: Elsie and Ella

Ella through her swollen dry throat, whispered "Elsie, me too."

Even in illness, Elsie and Ella were never apart. The September before, just after they turned twelve, Ella had suddenly collapsed to the ground. Her legs and back spasmed in pain. She could not climb upstairs, or get up the garden path to the toilet without toppling over. The doctor diagnosed TB of the spine, and that Ella was unlikely to recover or ever walk again. Ella slept a lot, was cheerful when with others, but often her pillow was wet with tears. Elsie cuddled up to her as they slept, or tried to keep Ella amused, by looking at photographs, reading to her, and playing cards. She wanted to leave school to look after Ella but her parents did not want Elsie to be glued to the sickroom. She would need other friends in the future.

George, their father, practical in crisis, took out their emergency savings, and even borrowed money for the first time, to buy a modern wheelchair with rubber wheels. He worked long hours of overtime, to pay off the debt and rebuild their savings, but also to avoid the pain of seeing Ella's constant struggle. Laudanum often had to be administered to Ella, whilst George escaped with an extra pint at the pub.

On good days, Elsie and her mother pushed Ella on riverside walks. Ella smiled as river breezes stroked her cheeks in summer and blew the cobwebs away in autumn: a relief from the still sickroom. Ella named the river birds, eider ducks, mute swans, herons, kingfishers, and Canadian geese. Elsie knew Ella was the clever one, and missed her help with arithmetic and nature study, when she was at school. They gathered elderflowers for wine, rosehips for cordial and sweet autumn blackberries. Last week their mother surprised them by shouting at the girls "Spit out the blackberries. it's past Michaelmas. They will be bitter. The devil will have weed on them and they're cursed."

On Sundays, Ella loved the services at Mistley Church, carried up the steps by their mother, who was small but strong willed. Emily was determined to include Ella in village life. In the candlelit church, Ella sniffed the scent of damp coats, polish, bees-wax melting, and fresh picked flowers, often wild, as garden flowers were mainly replaced by vegetables to provide extra food in wartime shortages. Ella joined in the hymns with as much vigour as her body permitted, and whispered the prayers. Emily remembered her angelic voice and rubbed her dry eyes. She had used up so many tears.

Elsie sat on the steps half way down the hall, where the house sloped down to the river bank, determined not to leave her sister. Whilst Emily was busy boiling water, Elsie crawled under the sheet hanging across the door, overpowered by the choking carbolic, and perched on Ella's temporary bed. Ella's eyes lit up at the boiled sweets. She sucked the orange and remembered tangerines at Christmas, nestled in the stocking with a sugar mouse, autograph book, and sewing kit. Ella could not swallow and passed Elsie the half sucked sweet to throw in the fire. Burnt toffee smell made both girls grin at their shared secret. As usual, Elsie told Ella the school gossip: Frank Seager had climbed over the manse wall to retrieve his football, got caught, and strapped by the school master. Football was forbidden so the girls enlarged their hopscotch and tied skipping ropes together to take over the playground. "We're suffragettes. We're in charge."
Frank Seager, facing the wall, led the chant "Girls can't skip, girls can't hop, girls can't kick a football. Rubbish."
Ella could still tease her sister "You like him. You'll get married."
"He makes me laugh, but he's even smaller than us."
As she fell asleep, Ella wheezed.

Emily knew Elsie had crept in to see Ella, and was torn. " George, the girls are inseparable, They belong together, but suppose Elsie became ill as well."
George carried a sleeping Elsie to her own bed. Emily settled to a bedside vigil. Ella weakened over the next two days. but still savoured the boiled fruit sweet tastes and memories: summer picnic strawberries, garden black currants, cherry pies, lemon barley, and roasted toffee apples from the fire. No bitter limes, just dreams of better times.

Ella sweated and shivered at the same moment, and prepared her mother for her death.
"I wouldn't like Flo not to get married in the Spring, because I died."
"You won't die, my love."
"I don't want a new fangled motor car for my funeral. Please can I have Midnight, the beautiful black horse, with feathers, and the hearse."

News travelled to Bradfield Rectory, where Bessie was cook, that Ella was ill. Mrs. Norman, the vicar's wife, let Bessie off her kitchen duties and sent her home to help. Bessie took over the cooking and cleaning, while Emily nursed

Ella. Practical Bessie bought sky blue wool to knit a cobweb shawl for Ella, and took turns to knit with Elsie. A race against time.

On October 20th, Bessie and Elsie gave Ella her shawl, and she stroked her face with the soft wool. That night, Emily watched by Ella's bed. Elsie crept in to bed with Ella when their mother dozed off. The two sisters wrapped their arms round each other, whole again. Later, George carried Elsie gently upstairs, then held Emily's hand. At dawn they opened the window for Ella's soul to soar with the flock of swans flying up through the river mists into the pink mackerel dawn sky. Elsie woke up in her own bed, her mother sitting still and silent beside her. "Ella's gone. The angels wanted her to join their choir."

Elsie and Bessie wrapped their shawl around Ella in the coffin, their last gift.

 Emily and George saved up for a white stone angel that cherished Ella's grave for thirty years. When George was dead, and Emily lost in senility in 1945, the angel disappeared overnight. Church authorities said it had become unsafe, and had to be removed, but Elsie and Flo feared the white angel was stolen for a grave in another churchyard

Auntie Elsie talked about Ella's last days in great detail, more often as she grew older, even when her short term memory had became muddled. Elsie missed Ella throughout her long life. Elsie's daughter, Val, reminded me of details like the boiled sweets, and the missing gravestone.

21: Auntie Elsie's Autograph Book

Auntie Elsie's autograph book
safe in cousin Val's memory box.
Red cloth covered, hand bound.
Paper measured, cut and folded,
stitched with a figure of eight.
Cow-glue spine wearing thin,
front cover loose, swinging free.
Family signed from World War One,
dated but now outside time.

Auntie Millie splashed her first wages,
on her twin sisters, ten years old.
"To Elsie with love, Xmas 1914".
Front page enshrined with pride,
no blots. A tidy pen dipped in ink.

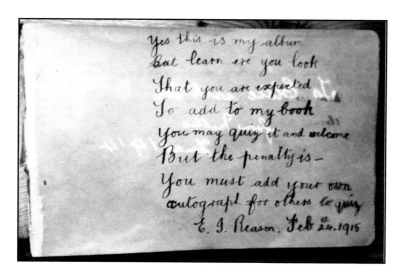

Followed by five family homilies
after Sunday dinner, February 24th 1915.
One with her mother Emily's wisdom

There is so much bad in the best of us,
And so much good in the worst of us
That it ill behoves any of us
To find fault with the rest of us." E.Reason 24/2/1915

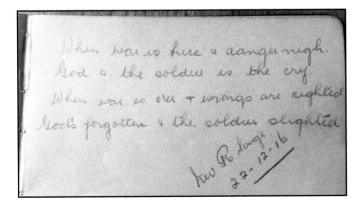

Sickness and war stifled autographs.
Twin sister Ella became wheelchair bound.
Then Nev, Flo's fiancé, wounded in Gallipoli,.
"When War is here and danger nigh,
God and the soldier is the cry.
When war is o'er and wrongs are righted,
God's forgotten and the soldier slighted."
Nev R Sage 22-12-16"

Elsie's book was closed by death and grief.
Sister's Ella and Bessie never grew old.
Time passed into a new generation.
Joan, Bessie's orphaned daughter, curious at nine,
opened her Auntie Elsie's sewing and treasure box
and happily, slipped in her skipping rhyme,
into the forgotten autograph book.

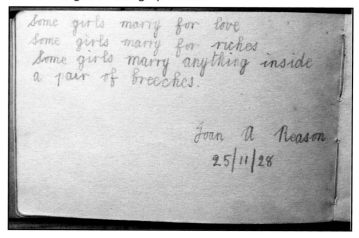

But instead of the expected laughter,
Nana and Auntie Elsie wept for their lost past.

My cousin Val and I found
our lost mothers, nanas and great-aunts,
grandads, fathers, and great-uncles
inside Elsie's autograph book.
Voices heard, love remembered,
memory wrapped in written words.
Past family forever around,
lost and found in and out of time,
stories from then, now and yet to come.

22: Bessie in the Cook House

Uniformed women marched up and down on the parade ground. Bessie painstakingly stepped forwards and backwards, clothes well brushed, shoes gleaming, and full of pride. She glanced at her new surroundings: rows of new wooden huts for the women, separated by a barbed wire fence from the men's quarters, of countless tents and huts. Standing to attention for inspection, Bessie smiled as the forewoman passed. Nearly six foot tall, short haired, with a faint moustache, she bellowed "Reason, wipe that smile off your face. You're not on a beauty parade, you're in the Women's Army Corps".

Bessie gritted her teeth, annoyed by the lack of encouragement, nothing was ever right. Bessie had imagined nursing the wounded, mopping fevered brows, handing tea to returning soldiers, transferring to France, but so far had only marched up and down, learning obedience. Why? Her standards were already high. Unlike the poorer girls, with colourless 'bread and jam' faces, who arrived with no underwear, and with stale, unwashed, permanent fishy time of month smells. Communal bathrooms with hot and cold taps, and carbolic soap had sweetened the air.

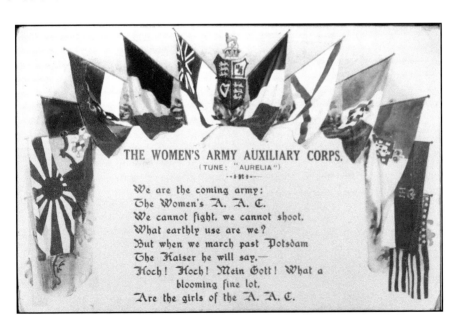

THE WOMEN'S ARMY AUXILIARY CORPS.

(TUNE: "AURELIA")

We are the coming army:
The Women's A. A. C.
We cannot fight, we cannot shoot,
What earthly use are we?
But when we march past Potsdam
The Kaiser he will say,—
Hoch! Hoch! Mein Gott! What a
blooming fine lot,
Are the girls of the A. A. C.

The new recruits found it difficult to leave the camp, because of the oversexed, over anxious male troops, keen to impress and for comfort from the storm; the smell of testosterone was overwhelming. On their first Saturday, Bessie and three new friends tried to go into Aldershot for egg and chips. They found themselves enclosed by a ring of soldiers, feeling for their breasts. Bessie's experiences of side-stepping Joseph, the chauffeur, gave her courage. "Keep walking girls. If you boys touch us, we'll report you and you'll be in the glass-house. I can read your cap badges, Private 4328 and 7369. Shame on you. We could be your sisters." The pack stood aside. Bessie shook with fear as she led her new friends out of the wolves den, and on to the cafe.

The hut was cold in the November damp; and the coke stove refused to draw and belched grey fumes. It was foggier inside than out. Forewoman Pritchard belted out "Open the windows."
As the women stood for inspection, they were hit by a cold blast. Bessie dared to speak, "Forewoman Pritchard, the flue needs cleaning, there's a birds' nest stuck inside."
"Are you complaining, Reason? Shall I get the chimney sweep for you? Soldier Reason, fetch a ladder and clear it." Bessie tucked her skirt up, climbed and put the cleared nest in the stove.
Bessie felt undervalued.

One morning at roll call, the forewoman bellowed "Two volunteers for the cook-house," Bessie stepped forward with Lily, a former chocolate factory worker from Birmingham. The cook-house, a permanent brick building stood in no-man's (or woman's) land, between the two camps with two parallel canteens, one for each sex, at each side. Bessie and Lily were the first women to work in the male staffed kitchen, and the banter momentarily stopped. The kitchen staff looked resentful; the women's army meant the men were more likely to be sent to the front. Rows of cooks peeled carrots, onions and swede for brown stew, simmering in giant pans, one with added spices and pepper for the newly arrived Indian troops. A Sikh hovered by the door, drawn by the hot humid air and smell of home. The door was quickly slammed in his face. Bessie was open mouthed at the rejection of the tall turbaned foreigner, unlike anyone she had ever met in her life.

Bessie was surprised by the breakfast cooking tricks; sausages pricked with a fork and boiled for five minutes before frying to make them edible, and rashers of bacon dipped in oatmeal to stop fat escaping and the bacon shrinking. The cook in charge approached "Either of you ladies know how to cook?"
Bessie stood tall "Yes, I am a cook, 7 years experience, cook in a rectory."
"We'll see. Here's the recipe for apple pie. Put on white overalls and hat, scrub your hands, and I'll show you the ingredients." Bessie was impressed by the array of sparkling pans, ovens and preparation tables. She quickly assessed the ingredients in the army recipe for apple pies for 100. 35lbs. of apples to be peeled, cut, put in pie dishes with 4lbs. of sugar and 60 cloves. Bessie turned boldly to the cook "Sergeant Field, 60 cloves will ruin the pies, 10 will be plenty".
"Reason, this is the army. You follow orders and recipes, but if you happen to miscount or misread the recipes, well it happens. But don't ever exceed the rations. Waste not, want not".

Lily fumbled with the peeler, cutting large chunks of apple. Bessie showed her an easier method, and they worked well together. Lily chatted about her four brothers, three in the army, and the younger one desperate to enlist, although he was only 13. Her mother wanted him never to get old enough, in short trousers for ever, but his voice was breaking. Bessie replied "I've got four sisters," then thought of Ella and a salt tear dripped on the apples. " Oh no. I've only got three sisters now. My little sister Ella only died last month with meningitis." Lily gently touched her arm, and Bessie talked fast to stop herself crying, "My sister Flo's getting married in March, but she's worried if Nev, her fiancé, will get back from the Balkans."
When the flour for the toppings arrived, Bessie blanched "I can't use heavy brown bread flour."
The porter smirked "That's what we've got in the stores."
Sergeant Field appeared instantly, aware of discord. "Causing trouble again Reason?"
Bessie reddened, but stood her ground "Is there any white flour? Why ruin good apple pies?"
"You're testing my limits, Reason."
Bessie felt she had lost all chance of working in the cook house again. "You're lucky not to be in Sussex, they're using mashed turnips instead of flour. You can mix half white in with the brown flour. You're baking for the troops not the vicar."

Bessie's card to her sister Elsie, includes

'Am very happy. Am in the cookhouse again today. I am the special one for the job so expect shall always get it. I don't mind as the cook tells me to go in for promotion so feel very pleased. No news of leaving here yet.'

Bessie and Lily prepared the pies, scrubbed the tables and peeled potatoes. When cook tried the first apple pie, he winked at Bessie approvingly. "Report here tomorrow and every day. You're the special one for the job. You could go in for promotion. Lily, you work hard and learn quickly. Report here as well." The two new recruits smiled, praised for the first time, since arriving in camp. "The sergeant is less bossy than our women foremen. They know what they're doing here." Lily laughed "It's because we're girls. The first to work in his kitchen. He's not sure how to treat us. None of his men would dare question the recipes. You weren't half lucky to get away with it."

Bessie , in uniform standing next to Elsie,
Behind Millie and Flo, right.
The four remaining sisters look subdued after Ella's death

23: Bessie meets Wiliam Aldridge

Bessie and Flo, arms interlinked to discourage pestering soldiers, turned towards Lyons Corner House on the Strand. These two tall, well rounded sisters chattered, one wearing Women's Army uniform; both in felt hats protecting shining long hair softly pinned up. Both with fresh complexions, though Bessie's face was overshadowed by black-ringed, shocked, tired eyes. They smiled sadly with relief at being together again. Two months since Ella's funeral, both had stoically tried to work as usual. But nothing would ever be the same, without their little sister. The cafe door opened to a blast of chatter, and hot steamy air. A short, pinch-faced nippy, in black and white laced uniform, hat falling over her eyes, glumly showed them to the end of a table occupied by six soldiers leering with high hopes. Both sisters asked for a quieter table, in unison. The nippy sighed, led them to a dark corner by the kitchen door. Flo laughed "They know where we belong. I'm surprised they don't expect us to start cooking."

The tension broken, the sisters silently colluded to ignore their grief and pretend life was normal. They focused on practicalities. Flo struggling to find good food for her rich South Kensington employers: slipping an extra threepence under the counter to the grocer for fresh eggs, and bribing the butcher with a cake to buy a leg of lamb. Flo turned green with envy as Bessie described the generous meat rations in Aldershot Barracks. "Nev is still fighting abroad; half-starving on Maconachie tinned stew in Macedonia." Flo could never resist a word play. "Mother's making me a black wedding dress, decorated with hand made lace. She wants to keep busy. We're hoping Nev will manage to be home for January, the banns will be read anyway, but I might be alone at the altar."
"It will work out. I so want to be at your wedding. Hope I can get leave. It doesn't look as though I'm going to France. Sergeant Field is eager to keep me in the cook house." At Flo's wink, Bessie gently kicks her "Not like that. He's a kind, stout middle aged married man".
Flo smiled, "They're the worst. Wolves in sheep's clothing. You always were gullible."
Both sisters were critical of the lunch: meatless sausages, chips swimming in grease, eggs small as pigeons', "Bet they gathered them in Trafalgar Square."

Sweet tea helped clear the taste. Bessie used the cafe toilets to avoid wriggling on the train. Their long goodbye hug contained all their loss and need for comfort. "Oh to be home at the Maltings, with all five of us girls together with mother and father, again."

Bessie crossed Hungerford Bridge, smiled at the orange glow of late autumn sunset over St Paul's but shivered as she walked alongside her dark shadow. Smuts and grey smoke shrouded Bessie, she hurried as the iron bridge juddered while a train crossed the river. Passing Lambeth Waterworks, soldiers jostled, women factory workers hurried home, shoulders hunched, coughing in the yellow mist, whilst prostitutes lingered in doorways, sporting red lipstick and rouge. Bessie strode hurriedly past, a wholesome country girl, head held high. Whilst juggling a large baby, a skeletal young woman begged for money. She shook a metal mug, containing two farthings in Bessie's face, Bessie felt uneasy in this dim, alien world. The infant whimpered, while her mother gazed into nothing. 'How could the poor girl have ended up so alone?' Bessie sadly dropped a penny in the chipped enamel mug.

The tunnel to Waterloo Station stenched of dead animal skins from the steaming tannery, and Bessie retched. Troops bustled past, pinched her bottom, and groped for her breasts. Alone, assaulted and scared, Bessie rushed up the steps, brushing tears and soldiers away, emerging into concourse chaos. A Scots pipe band of proud frightened boys marched towards a one way train to the Front, passing stretchers returning with bandaged bodies. The departures board clattered the wooden display and Bessie headed to the Aldershot train. Tempted at the news-stand by an amusing postcard and a penny dreadful to lift her spirits. She hurried past the free station buffet for troops, past soldiers and girlfriends posing for last photos together. Alone and overwhelmed.

Soldiers pushed into the carriages and Bessie hunted for one containing other women. A glimpse of a chaplain in dog collar offered a promise of security. But on clambering into the compartment, the reverend's inverted eyes, grey skin, stray hairs and whiskers on his bald head gave no reassurance, even less so when he twisted a finger in his waxy ear. Bessie stepped over the disappointing cleric to the far window seat, and secretly wiped a tear away. A sergeant sat down in the middle seat opposite. Bessie assessed his reflection in the window: mid thirties, blond wavy hair and moustached, and caught his eye as he half smiled. Beware of wolves that shave off their hair in disguise. A predator lurks inside. Bessie averted her eyes

At the last moment three troopers jumped in the compartment,

I'VE JUST ARRIVED

AT SARRATT

breathing beer fumes, tripping over each other into the empty seats. Blowing her nose, Bessie looked absently at her magazine, and longed to be going home. The last straw, the fat ruddy soldier opposite, rubbed his muddy boot up her leg. Bessie kicked him away, as the observant Sergeant leapt to her defence, "You're annoying the lady, exchange places."

Bessie felt reassured by the friendly sergeant, "I'm William Aldridge. Are you alright miss? You look sad." A gentleman. At his kindness Bessie's tears flowed, blurting out her story "My little sister died three months ago. I really miss my family. I just met my sister Flo for lunch." William listened

80

attentively, told Bessie he had just escorted his sister, from Brighton, to see Buckingham Palace. At Aldershot, Bessie felt safe when he offered to walk her back to camp in the dark, and took her arm. He held her close, and Bessie glowed. At the gate William smartly saluted, and they arranged to meet at the tea shop the next Saturday. Bessie grinned at the unexpected outcome of her journey. Her postcard to Flo reflects her new optimism. William tweaked his moustache ends.

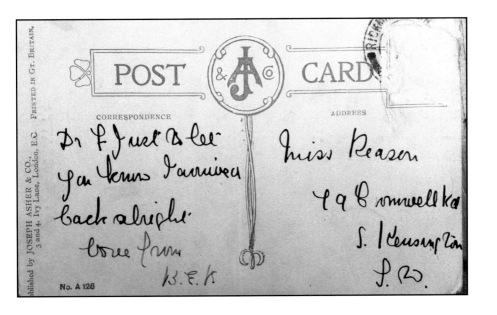

24: Soldier, soldier, won't you marry me?

Bessie tore open the long awaited letter from William, but, after reading a few lines, the words became blurred by tears. 'Darling Bessie. I love you very much, but I am sorry, I wan't honest. I'm already married, and cannot desert my wife... ' Bessie screwed up the letter, and stared into nothing. He was married, and had lived a double life. Cheated on his wife, while courting Bessie in Aldershot. Her dreams splintered. It was all a lie. The old playground song drummed in her head:

> "Soldier, soldier, won't you marry me?
> With your musket, pipe and drum
> Oh no, fair maid, I cannot marry you.
> For I have a wife of my own"

A year of love, support and joy soured into bitter truth. All became clear. William's reluctance to meet her family, his frequent weekend leaves in Brighton to visit his supposed sister. He had obviously gone home to his wife. The reason he dragged Bessie away from an accidental meeting in Piccadilly with his old workmate became apparent. Alfred had leered through narrow eyes, and thumped William on his back "Enjoying yourself Will? Never knew you had it in you."
Bessie had felt cheapened "What's he implying?"
"Oh, he's just jealous, Alf never had any luck with the ladies."

William's transfer to France had arrived back in February. But no marriage proposal. "We'll wait until I return. I don't want you to be a widow. You know I'll always love you."

Bessie had shivered. William might die without knowing how much she loved him. She would be a spinster, living with the dreams of a cold frigid past. Instead of pushing William away as he reached to stroke her breasts, she melted towards him. The logistics office, full of maps and train timetables, became a palace, as they slid off his chair, and merged into one another on the scorched grey rug in front of the smoking coke stove. 'Why had she waited for such delight?' Warm waves, laughter, rolling over, khaki uniforms and buttons fumbled, becoming whole. What joy. They lay back and grinned at each other.

William showered her face, her half exposed breasts, and tickled her strong thighs with kisses, and they joined again, two parts of a jigsaw puzzle.

For a week before he departed, they had spent every early evening locked in the communications office. When Bessie crept back to her hut. Lily looked knowingly at her "You're glowing Bessie, overtime in the cook-house again? Careful you don't get a bun in the oven." How coarse. Bessie had held her head high, enmeshed in a spider's web of warm deceptive love.

Bessie had thought they would get engaged before he left for the front, but William had still wanted to wait for the war's end. "Why?" William's eyes narrowed, "Are you questioning my love?" Seeds of doubt were planted, but Bessie buried them deep inside. William left. Loving letters flowed. Then lack of her monthly bleed, and tingling breasts revealed the truth. William would be delighted, surely? They would marry. She wrote with the good news.

No reply came. But William's letters were not lost in the post. William did not reply for three months, out of cowardice and guilt. But he was not, as Bessie feared, dead.

Stunned by the contents of the long awaited letter, Bessie lay under her blankets in the darkened barrack room What a fool. William had deceived her. Why was she so stupid? The night before, she had stroked her rounded stomach. Bessie had imagined marrying, her parents welcoming William and their baby. Now she would be shamed, rejected, end up in the work-house. William's letter shocked her. He loved Bessie, but he was married. Bessie shuddered in disbelief. William's wife was sickly, and could not have children. He could not leave this good woman. He had admitted everything to his wife, and she would forgive him, but he must never see Bessie again. Bessie choked back her sobs: he had even written to his wife first, before her. William wrote that he regretted their passion, but Bessie had tempted him with her kindness in the lonely barracks, with her hot apple pies, and her warm body. He promised to send money for the confinement.

Not her hero after all, just a coward.

Rejected, Bessie no longer wanted this baby.

What would mother and father say?
Where could she go?   Bessie slept fitfully. Lost and alone.

Then her baby butterflied inside her womb...

25: Bessie falls from grace

George blustered, stumbled up
volcanic puce face,
stone voice.
Geyser steamed,
anger fuelled.
"I earn the bread, head this house.
Wage earner for a tribe
of women
lacking any respect.
I worked my way up from nothing:
a human scarecrow in the fields.
Now, I'm foreman of the Maltings,
studied science at night school,
can measure specific density.
Do you even know what that is?

Smell and feel when grain is ready,
manage a barrel full of maltsters.
All obey me, jump when I move.
They respect my every word.

Emily, you mothered disorder.
Birth to one daughter after another.
Why could you not give me sons?
I taught your daughters manners.
Only Ella and Elsie respected me.
But our little angel was stolen,
replaced
by a graveyard stone statue.
Our dear Ella cold and dead.
I am a valued church warden, yet
not respected by wife or daughters.
Bessie is the whore of Babylon,
a fallen woman, carrying a bastard:

fornicated with a married man.
No morals, no common sense.
Cooked for the rector, but left
to be a ruddy woman soldier.
Wearing trousers next, no shame.
Brought our family into dishonour."

Emily glanced over her glasses,
bitterly darning George's socks.
"Oh you've paused for breath.
Remember husband
I was with child when we married.
You were no saint. You rushed me.
Even fined once for illegal drinking:
judged and named in the paper.
You hypocrite, you shame me.
Where is your Christian kindness?"

George's pipe fumed smoke signals,
prepared for the oncoming battle.
"Bessie will not darken my doorstep,
overblown, bearing her bastard.
Once that baby is born, they
can only return after dark.
I've risen from nothing
I will not be shamed by....."

Emily threw down flawless socks,
rose up to full five feet and
towered over her giant husband.
"For once this is not about you.
Our daughter, and grandchild
will not end up rejected,
hidden away in the workhouse.
Bessie is loving, gentle, soft,
now betrayed, sad and lost.
We will welcome her home.
Remember love and forgiveness."
George grew silent, shamed,
frozen in cold anger, flustered.

26: Bessie's banishment. September 1918

Blankets torn off her foetal sleep,
Bessie stirred from deep dreams,
dragged into a dawn nightmare.
"Stand to attention, Worker Reason.
Not just been eating well, have we?"
From the next-door barrack room bed,
wide-eyed, Lily peered out, dumbfounded.

Forewoman Pritchard barked
"Shame on you, Reason.
You deceived us all, you slut."
Bessie's mind wandered,
pictured slut's wool under slovenly beds.
Bessie stood majestic, maternal,
shivering in early autumn cold,
and swallowed down her distress.

Forewoman Pritchard lifted
Bessie's virginal white nightie,
to reveal cloth wound round,
to hide Bessie's secret shame.
Forewoman Pritchard's eyes
gleamed, suspicions validated.
She pulled the bandages binding
Bessie's blooming stomach.
Bessie planted her feet firmly,
but forceful unwinding
still twisted her around.
Bessie's unbound pod swelled,
revealing joyous baby kicks,
playful in newly extended room.
Determined not to cry, Bessie
pulled her nightie down,
and stood defiant, a Madonna

in dishevelled blanket pile.
"Don't speak to anyone,
Dress in civilian clothes.
Fold your uniform on the bed.
Pack up all your belongings.
Report to me in 30 minutes."

As the outside door slammed,
Bessie, a shocked statue,
cried silent, shamed tears.
Lily leapt out of bed, and
hugged her cookhouse friend.
All offered Bessie comfort,
though secretly grinned at
gossiped suspicions confirmed.
Bessie dressed in let out skirt,
loose blouse, best jacket,
buttons undone, no hat.
No protection from life's storms.
uniform greatcoat abandoned.
Lily helped pack her bag: bible,
recipe book, letters, mirror, brush,
baby clothes made pretending
sister Flo was expecting.
Bed stripped, uniform laid out,
her roommates wished Bessie well,
as she stepped into the unknown,
head held high, smiling goodbye,
from her tear washed face, Aware
of her baby, dancing in new found freedom.

27: Bessie in Kilburn

Bessie panicked out of underground hell,
panting, sure her kit bag would be stolen
by the beer fuelled Tommy,
who'd offered to carry her bag
up countless curving stairs.
He was waiting, grinning
"Good luck, lass. Turn left."
Her last hope destination appeared:
"Queen Charlotte Convalescent Home"
drab, brown paint, four stories high,
with institutional, uncleaned,
smeared windows.

Eight steep steps to the sad front door.
Buffeted by traffic noise, shouts and echoes,
Bessie drooped, dragged herself upwards,
red faced, heart throbbing, sweat pouring.
Rejected by William, father, the WAAC,
alone, longing for a warm welcome,
Bessie pulled at the door bell.
Nothing.

Far away, a voice echoed from below,
"Come down into the basement."
Shell shocked, down into hell?
Scramble, stumble, overladen.
Wide open door into a warm kitchen.
Clean, gleaming china, scrubbed table.
Greeted by a smiling robust girl,
as round with pregnancy as short.
"Sit down, cup of char? I'm Lou.
You're cream crackered."

Tall in well tailored navy dress,
in pristine apron, scowling
appeared the pinched matron,
who, coldly, challenged Bessie,
in strident, accusatory tones.
"Where have you turned up from?
We have no room for stray alley cats."
Bessie choked on her tea, tears flowed,
"I have a referral letter from the WAAC."
Jane Kistruck scanned it closely,
Her eyes widened, almost smiled,
"You cook?
Everyone pulls her weight here.
We are called a rest home, but
there is no rest for the wicked."
A joke or condemnation?
Unsure, Bessie pondered,
spotted burnt currant buns.

Bessie retorted. "I am a good cook.
Cooked in Bradfield Vicarage for 8 years.
A hard worker. Are you from Suffolk?"
Miss Kistruck peered back, surprised.
"Your accent. I'm from Mistley."
"We do have space for a cook.
Louise, show her to your room,
Make porridge at six in the morning."
Bessie became an unpaid skivvy,
cook for the mother and baby home
busy baking for the next twelve weeks:
grateful not to be walking the streets.

28: Walnut cake
November 11th 1918

"A woman, a dog, a walnut tree,
the more they're beaten the better they'll be."

Hidden in next-door's abandoned garden,
three overblown foragers sang loud and free.
Bessie, Polly and Lou battered the groaning tree,
beat in rhythmic tune with snapped off branches.
Grey anger vented, orange laughter released.
Half husked walnuts rattling down,
final shellfire of a wilting war.

Veteran walnuts fell on withered leaves.
Squirrels scavenged the dropped shells,
speedy thieves storing nuts in pantry holes.
Bessie, Polly and Lou wobbled down,
to glean the scattered walnuts:
tumbling unbalanced clowns,
pods over stretched, baby full,
autumn harvests of spring sowing.
Shamed, judged for too kind love.

Nuts gathered in rough jute bags,
ready to husk and shell
for Bessie to bake a walnut cake.
War discord split the garden calm:
rockets boomed, "an attack warning!
But they're having peace talks!"
Roosting pigeons swarmed, circled,
retreated home. Bessie jumped,
landed on a puff ball, released
dry fungus dust, a stench of death.

Silence echoed. More rocket fire.
Bessie, Polly and Lou clung together.
Sudden shouts of joy "War's over.."
Cheers of relief. News of peace
spread like Wildfire from the West End.
Church bell clamour. Shock. Smiles.
Flag wavers danced the hokey cokey.

Bessie, Polly and Lou wept in joy,
circled, cheered, hugged; outcasts,
war's flotsam. Crept invisible
up the overgrown side passage,
back to the mother and baby home.
Forbidden to display their shame.
but joyful with their secret harvest,
they sat down round the basement table,
to drink a victory cup of sweet tea.

Wet walnut husks removed,
Well worn fingers stained brown.
Walnut shells, like small grenades
splintered. Nut shards exploded out,
bursting with woodland taste.
Bessie produced her recipe book,
pages turned, admired by all,
Mouths watered over unimagined feasts.

Bessie's recipe 144: Walnut cake
1/2lb flour, 4ozs castor sugar,
whites of 4 eggs, vanilla essence
Cream the butter and sugar, add flour, walnuts, and whites of eggs beaten
stiffly.
Bake in moderate oven 3/4 hour

Bessie magicked a changeling cake.
No butter, just wartime margarine, but
grated carrot and apple added for moisture.
Four beaten egg whites unavailable,
only two eggs and bicarbonate of soda.
Rough brown flour. No vanilla essence,
coffee stirred in to enhance the taste.
A tray of quickly roasted walnuts added.
A celebration cake for hidden victims of war.
Punished, gazing at dancing boots through
smeared windows of their basement jail,
whilst nurturing the nation's future children.

"A woman, a dog, a walnut tree,
The less they're beaten, the happier they'll be."

Women from the WAAC march in victory celebrations

143. Biscuits

6 ozs flour, 4 ozs butter 4 ozs castor sugar, whites of 2 eggs well beaten, flour flavouring. Mix well with a little milk if required, roll out to about ¼ inch in thickness, and cut in fancy shapes. Place on greased paper and bake in a moderate oven and bake each side a pale brown

---

144 Walnut Cake.

½ lb flour, 4 ozs castor sugar, 4 ozs butter, 4 ozs chopped walnuts, 4 whites eggs, vanilla essence. Cream the butter and sugar, add flour, walnuts etc whites of eggs beaten stiffly. Bake in moderate oven ¾ hour.

---

145 Fruit Cake.

1 lb flour, ½ lb butter, 6 ozs castor sugar, 2 ozs ground almonds, 2 ozs sweet almonds, ¼ lb glace cherries, ¼ lb citron peel, 1 teaspoonful baking powder, 3 eggs, 1 tablespoon milk. Blanch and slice almonds, cut peel into strips and cherries into quarters. Whip the eggs well, whites and yolks separately. Sift flour into a basin adding baking powder. Rub the butter in lightly, stir in almonds peel and cherries. Mix with the yolks of eggs & lastly the whites & milk.
Bake 1½ hours

95

29: Bessie gives birth

Stories that hide the truth

My mother, Joan, never forgave her mother, Bessie. "I was illegitimate. Not only that my mother died and I was an orphan as well. I was different from my cousins." No photos of Bessie existed in our house, no mention ever made of my grandparents. Bessie was a hidden secret, a lost grandmother. I only knew that I was forbidden to ride a bicycle, because my grandmother had died in a bicycle accident. Grandparents were alien to me, enjoyed by other children. Bessie's absence consumed a large space. Bessie's sisters, my great aunts, Flo, Millie and Elsie provided a loving and supportive, replacement trio. When Auntie Flo showed me a large framed photo of her sister, Bessie, my mother's lips tightened, and she marched off to the outside loo, on her well polished court shoes. Bessie was not an embarrassment for her sisters, but a well remembered, loved and lively woman.

My mother's account of her birth was sketchy. Joan believed Bessie went to stay with Auntie Millie's friend Edie Hawkins in East London, after she left the Women's Army. Joan believed she was a Cockney, born within the sound of Bow Bells. This myth provides hope with suggestion of friendly support, comforted by chiming bells.

None of this oral story was true, probably invented to hide the bitter reality of Bessie's rejection. My research shows Bessie, pregnant, dismissed from the WAAC, alone, abandoned by both William and her father. She was not staying with family friends, but forced to live in an institution for unmarried mothers.

Uncovering the facts.

My mother's birth certificate was a short version, just containing her name, Joan Aldridge Reason, and date of birth, 8th December 1918. When I sent for a full version 10 years ago, I received another short version. No progress. After we celebrated Joan's centenary in December 2018, I decided to tackle the birth certificate issue again, as many restrictions are lifted after 100 years. With my best headteacher's voice, I phoned the GRO, and ordered a full certificate. After interrogation, the helpful young man patiently reassured me three times that I would receive a full certificate, within 21 days.

Support from Edie Hawkins.
Meanwhile, my detective skills turned to finding Edie Hawkins, where Bessie was supposed to have stayed. My mother's photo album contained a photo of Auntie Millie and Edie, middle aged with Millie, on the left, dressed in a wrap-round pinny. (The spell checker keeps replacing pinny, obviously an archaic word now, with penny or pinky)

I searched all the appropriate aged Edie or Edith Hawkins living in London, in the 1911 census, focusing on the East End because of the Bow Bells cockney myth. I looked for women born within five years of 1895, roughly the same age as Auntie Millie. Eighteen Edith Hawkins were available to choose from the Ancestry 1911 census index. A startling number. At first I focused on possible East Enders.
However, at this point, my mother's full birth certificate arrived.

97

CERTIFIED COPY OF AN ENTRY OF BIRTH — GIVEN AT THE GENERAL REGISTER OFFICE

Application Number 9953017-1

REGISTRATION DISTRICT — ST. MARYLEBONE

1918 BIRTH in the Sub-district of St. Mary in the County of London

Eighth December 1918 Queen Charlotte's Hospital — Joan Aldridge — Girl — Bessie Emma Reason cook (w.a.a.b.) Manningtree — B.E. Reason mother The Maltings Manningtree Essex — Twelfth December 191 8 — G.W. Bassett Deputy Registrar

...FIED to be a true copy of an entry in the certified copy of a Register of Births in the District above mentioned.

...the GENERAL REGISTER OFFICE, under the Seal of the said Office, the 4th day of March 2019

734543

CAUTION: THERE ARE OFFENCES RELATING...

One myth quickly dispelled. Joan Aldridge Reason was not a Cockney. She was born at Queen Charlotte's Hospital, Hammersmith. Bessie's address was given as The Maltings, Manningtree, Essex. No clue to where Bessie was staying pre-birth. Was Bessie even helped by Edie Hawkins?

My 1911 census search focussed on Hammersmith. Eureka! the most likely was:

NAME:	Edith Laura Jane Hawkins
ADDRESS:	13 Paradise Row. Hammersmith
PARENTS:	Albert Hawkins, horse dealer and Mary Hawkins, Edith was 2nd of 8 children
OCCUPATION:	Lamp maker at Osrams

Auntie Millie worked at Osrams but not until the 1930s, so it seems unlikely that she knew Edie in 1918. They probably became friends later when they worked together. Bessie was unlikely to have stayed in an already crowded 13 Paradise Row.

Hospital record revelations

London Metropolitan Archives could provide detailed information about Joan's birth, from the records of Queen Charlottes Hospital, as she was born more than 100 years ago.   In order to receive the details, I had to confirm the dates of death of Joan and Bessie. The hospital transcription reads

MOTHER			
Name	Bessie Reason	Midwife	Wilson
Residence	20 Victoria Rd Kilburn	Presentation	Vertex
Religion	C of E	Delivery	Normal
Admission number	1422	Discharge	17 Dec 1918
Age	24	Condition on Leaving	Good
Civil status	Single	Length of stay	10 days
Previous Pregnancies	None		
Admission	8 Dec 1918: 5am		
Delivery	8 Dec 1918: 10.30am		

CHILD			
Sex	F	Date of discharge	17 Dec 1918
Born dead or alive	Alive	Condition on leaving	Good
Apparent Age	Premature	Length of stay	10 days
Weight at birth	6lb 3oz	Condition on leaving	Good

Bessie's current address was 20 Victoria Road, Kilburn. On my first glance at the 1911 census, it housed a long list of single women. Alarm bells rang. Had Bessie been forced to stay in a brothel? Most of the women were aged 20 to 30. Was Jane Kistruck, aged 46, the madam? However, it was quickly apparent that most of the women had a baby born in 1911, and were staying in a mother and baby home, Jane Kistruck was described as "Matron of a convalescent home." Queen Charlotte's Convalescent Home was a temporary refuge for girls with their first child, who had nowhere to go and were still too weak to look after themselves. *(Fagin's children, Jeannie Duckworth).*

Attitudes to unmarried mothers were changing in WW1. Although there was still a double set of moral standards for men and women. Illegitimate mothers were either judged harshly as sinners or as needing support. In the Guardian 25 April 1915, a report read:
"*With the establishment of military camps all over the country, a very large number of illegitimate children must be the children of soldiers.*
It is said that the number of illegitimate births per annum is 36,000.
Mrs. Arnold Glover, secretary of the National Union of Girl's clubs said "Problem is not a working class trouble only. The temptation was one which undoubtedly

women of all classes had been subjected. Working class women came into prominence simply through the problem of affording their financial support. It is hoped that suitable provision would be made for the mothers, not only in special lying in hospitals, but also providing suitable paid employment before and after the child's birth. Most of the girls are now going through a time of INTENSE UNHAPPINESS AND FINANCIAL STRESS. They would not return to their old employment, but hide themselves away...Although with an open air life and an opportunity to care for their baby....they would learn to love their babies, otherwise the obvious danger was that they would regard them with horror".

Many unmarried mothers were forced to give up their babies for adoption. Many people believed the children should be adopted by respectable parents who could provide a good home. Mothers were often extremely distressed after the enforced separation. Some of the mothers were sent to mental asylums, and left institutionalised: only discovered after 50 years, when the Care in the Community Act came into force.

It was a struggle for single women to bring up children. The National Council for Unmarried Mothers, created in 1918, aimed to keep children with their mothers.

.Bessie's life reflects the complex emotional and social problems of a chaotic post wartime society.

Leaflets for Letters, (Gospel, No. 37.)

"WHY NOT TO-NIGHT?"

On! do not let the word depart,
And close thine eyes against the light.
Poor sinner, harden not thy heart:
  Thou wouldst be saved—Why not to-
    night?

To-morrow's sun may never rise
  To bless thy long-deluded sight;
Now is the time. Oh, then, be wise!
  Thou wouldst be saved—Why not to-
    night?

Our God in pity lingers still;
  And wilt thou thus His love requite?
Renounce, at length, thy stubborn will:
  Thou wouldst be saved—Why not to-
    night?

The world has nothing left to give—
  It has no new, no pure delight;
Oh! try the life which Christians live:
  Thou wouldst be saved—Why not to-
    night?

I found this underlined tract buried inside Bessies confirmation bible, addressed to "A Poor Sinner". Bessie probably judged herself harshly

30: Afterbirth: Queen Charlotte's Hospital
December 1918

Mother and child cradled together,
in the hard hospital nursing chair,
lost in a long regimented line,
breast feeding timed like clockwork,
overseen by pristine uniformed nurses.
Bessie stroked her daughter's round cheek,
Joan nuzzled towards her mother's breast:
downy white haired, plum blue eyed,
direct stare, critical, quizzical "Why?"
An old soul, bearing wisdom and innocence.
Joan was an unwanted gift, rejected
by her father and grandparents,
Bessie gently kissed her crown,
"I have to love you. No one else will."

Joan's new born scent was fading,
bleached away by hospital soap.
Nurse's starched apron crackled
"Miss Reason, time to change sides."
Timetables ruled, must avoid attachment,
A greedy queue of childless parents
hammered at the maternity ward doors,
waiting to adopt into respectable homes.
Joan deepened her gaze, entreated love.
Bessie softly laid Joan in her iron crib,
"I am your mother. I will find a solution."

Alone in the crowded cheerless ward,
Bessie read her bible for solace.
No wise men to welcome her babe,
No Joseph to find a smelly stable.
Absent William was comfy with his wife.
No bright star, angels or shepherds.

No joy for Joan's birth, just isolation.
In the next door bed, Lou wept, bereft.
Baby George removed by robber parents.
Bessie's words of sympathy rejected.
Lou turned her back, inconsolable.
"I will keep Joan. But how?"

Covers pulled straight, hair brushed
for invisible visitors, who never materialised.
The ward's dour doors swung open,
filled by Flo, secure, tall and strong.
Bright hawk eyes scanning the beds,
searching, set smile, determined.
Flo swept down the ward, successful.
Ample bosom hugs, Bessie inhaled fresh air.
"Well, look at you, Princess Bessie,
Laying in bed, not hospital cook by now?
Lazy bones." Bessie relaxed at last,
smiled. Unshed tears flooded her bed.
"They want Joan to be adopted.
I'll run away with her, and hide."

Resourceful Flo had the remedy.
"There's another visitor. Are you ready?"
Mother dusted in, bearing love, and solutions.
"Father's seen sense and relented.
We want you and Joan to come home.
to celebrate Christmas all together.
Although you must arrive after dark."
Bessie recognised a half hearted gesture,
"Anything, to bring Joan safely home."
"Bessie, my love, where is Joan?
They separate you? That's not on."

Mother, Bessie and Flo gazed at Joan,
shaking her fists, trembling, in tears.
Divided by a cold polished window, family

reflections mingled with their crying child.
Bessie's milk flowed, Emily responded,
"Joan needs a cuddle, she's all alone,"
Emily tugged at the heavy nursery door,
swept in, small in height, yet towering tall,
picked up her grandchild, cuddled her close.
Nurses swooped, alarmed by the intruder.
Emily gently kissed Joan, settled her down,
returned, scooped up Bessie with a hug,
held her lost and found daughter securely
"Bessie, dear, when can you come home?"

31: Bessie at the station

The whistle blasted out her arrival, an owl hooted, denouncing her sin, echoed by the baby screeching her presence in the wicker basket. Mists drifted from the river weaving a cover across Manningtree station, mixing with the smoke of the 4.45 arrival. Doors crashed open. Bessie hid inside her hooded coat, and climbed down with her base-born basket into the gloom. 'No one would know her, no-one would meet her." Hidden under layers of crochet covers and knitted blankets, baby Joan trumpeted her birth and her mother's shame.

Bessie found herself face to face with Mrs. Kensit-Norman, who had savoured Bessie's cooking in her vicarage kitchen, praised her Queen of Puddings. Mrs. Kensit-Norman gave her glowing references to join the Woman's Army and support the war effort. Now, she looked past Bessie, denying her presence, before wafting into the cloud of belching smoke.

Doors shut and the train clattered across Judas's Gap towards Harwich.

Passengers gossiped and picked their way down the icy steps, threatening disaster. An empty platform, apart from Bessie and her bundle, disappearing in a fresh drift of sleep, and an anxious looking station master. He recognised despair. Kind words: "Let me help you down the stairs, Miss".
'Doesn't he know I'm an outcast, a returning leper, rejected by my family?'
No one was there to meet her.

Stumbling up the stairs, towards the exit, revealed by the glow of the station buffet, Bessie contemplated diverting into the misty fields rather than the long march to her father's judgement. Running footsteps clinked in hurry "Bessie, Bessie, Let's see Joan.' Enveloped by her bouncing sister, Elsie, and a warm hug from her mother, closely followed by big sister Flo, "See, you're both home for Christmas."

Emily beamed at her first grandchild, her first joy since Ella's death. Flo in mourning had even married in black. Elsie had not smiled since she climbed into bed with her twin sister to hold her as she drifted away. "Oh Bessie she's lovely, can I help you to carry her home?" They chattered in old tunes, but as they turned the last corner they were silent, drowned in cold and dark river mists.

A strident bicycle bell rang an alarm and the butcher's boy skidded across the road just missing the regiment of women. A swan ghosted across the sky. An omen? Bessie trembled, 'Will father send us to the workhouse?' The back gate creaked a new discordant hymn of shame and disgust. Flo put her arm around her shivering sister.

> 80 years later, Great Auntie Elsie repeated her well-sung story, silent tears falling in memory. "We were all scared, we didn't know what father would say. He rose from his wooden chair, and said "Poor little mite. She must be frozen give her to me to toast by the fire. He stood up and reached out for Joan"

Glancing at the daughter who he often ignored, George was shocked by her tear and soot stained face. Bessie had been the most robust of his daughters, always sunny side-up. He had just lost one daughter, he feared for this newly thin spectre. His pre-conceived judgement faltered "Welcome home, Bessie." He would countenance no more lost daughters.

32: Christmas Eve 1918

Hidden away upstairs, Bessie gently covered Joan's fragile shell ears, to deafen the chicken's screams. Joan nuzzled into her mother's bounteous bosom, oblivious to the carnage outdoors.

Nev, the chosen slaughterer, lowered the axe. But injured, the chicken flapped away, knocked flower pots over, fluttered futile wings in a last escape attempt, and stone-like fell on the Brussel sprouts. Nev wiped away a single tear, 'yet more bloody carnage.' Hoarse coughing from trench gas racked his body. Flo hugged her tormented husband, entrapped her broken hero in warm love. Nev treasured the moment, but defensive reactions won the day. He detached himself, soldier-style. Quickly, mounted his bike, and rode away to hunt out horseradish roots in roadside ditches: an escape from witnessing Flo gutting and plucking the sacrificial hen. He felt suffocated, overwhelmed by womanly gentle love, which battled in his heart with ever-present echoes of war. He missed Barrack-room humour: protective detachment from feelings. Every night he wandered amongst dead friends on the battle field, and pushed Flo away as she tried to wake him up, while he screamed "Watch out." Too late.

Elsie carried warm sweet tea up to Bessie, and cuddled Joan, whilst Bessie dressed; her pre-Army tops no longer fitted, so she wore Flo's larger borrowed blouse. Still she diligently brushed her hair 50 times, determined not to be defined by her father's judgement as a "slut."

Before Aunt Maria was due to visit, George ordered Bessie to take Joan upstairs. Maria marched into the kitchen, resplendent in Edwardian black cape and long silk skirt (my dressing up clothes 40 years later). Maria, a match for her puffed-up younger brother, settled down in his fireside chair, and heard kitten cries from above. "I've come to see Bessie and your granddaughter. Why are they upstairs? Be more forgiving George. Value your treasures." George silently strode off to the pub. Maria crossed her great-niece's palm with silver, and hugged Bessie, who wept, grateful for her aunt's acceptance.

Later Bessie and Elsie made mince pies together, kneading, rolling, and cutting. Mother opened her pantry, groaning with blackberry jam, crab-apple and medlar jelly, pickled onions and walnuts, but with only one jar of mincemeat, and a small Christmas Pudding. Emily knew how to make-do with food still rationed. "It's still impossible to buy dried fruit, we'll use apples as well." She burrowed for Bramley apples, wrapped in newspaper and stored under the bed in September. Bessie peeled, chopped and stewed the fruit with cinnamon and cloves, glad to be cooking again. They spooned mincemeat into half the batch and spiced apples in the remainder. Elsie chattered nonstop. Emily smiled to see her lost daughter happy again, after two silent years since Ella's death. Baby Joan had restored life into the house.

Millie arrived on the afternoon bus. Granted two days off from her kitchen duties at Kingsford Hall. She had bought South African oranges from the market in Colchester High Street, as she changed buses. Reunited, the four sisters group hugged. Millie turned her attention to her new niece, and smiled, "Bessie, she's beautiful. It's good to see you both." She lifted Joan, from her basket, who looked her aunt up and down. Millie chatted non-stop. "Who does Joan look like? She's got blue eyes? Does she take after her father?"
Bessie chortled, "Millie, only you could manage to put your big size 8 feet right in it. I do love you, but you need to think before you speak. Good job father's out."
As Joan wriggled, Millie quickly handed her back.

Millie suddenly pulled off her cloche hat. All eyes turned to stare at her newly shorn hair. Emily gasped "What will your father say."
"Everyone's getting short hair. It's the new fashion."
 Flo knew she would never cut her mane of long hair. "Short hair styles will cost you money all your life. You'll always be at the hair-dressers."

After tea, George escaped to the pub again, with his son-in-law; whilst the women chatted non-stop and prepared vegetables, ready for Christmas dinner, and laid out bread, cheese and pickles for supper after midnight mass. Four good cooks jostled for position. Bessie had spotted the oranges, and convinced mother to let her make Orange Mould, ready for Christmas Day tea, delighted to use her treasured recipe book again. Elsie peeled the oranges and copied the recipe.

Recipe 69: Orange Cream (idea) Elm Lodge
2 oranges rubbed with18 lumps of sugar, put on to boil
with juice of oranges & 1 lemon, add a little less than
1/2 oz. of gelatine. When nearly cold add 1/2 cream & mould

Millie gossiped loudly " Our new kitchen-maid can't even boil an egg. Thirteen years old. Fresh from the work-house."
Mother quietly interrupted "Think how the poor girl feels, Millie. Imagine growing up with no family and no experience of home cooking."

Apart from Bessie and baby Joan, the whole family set off to walk joyfully along the windswept riverside to Mistley church for Midnight Service. Wrapped in scarves and hats, carrying oil lights and acetylene bicycle lamps, Millie's voice rang out in competition with the church bells, as she greeted old friends.

Back at home, Bessie felt abandoned, she had always loved the candlelight service. Her father was busy publicly praising a virgin mother and baby, whilst he ignored his own unmarried daughter. He had avoided looking at her, though at least he seemed to dote on his first grandchild.

Joan whimpered, and Bessie lifted up her hungry baby. "We'll get through this together. It will all work out."

33: In the workhouse in 1919

Bessie felt torn in two, as they drove up the long tree lined drive to Tendring Workhouse. Her father silent, still disapproving.

Tendring Workhouse

Bessie would miss Joan so much, but £35 a year wages as cook would help to pay her way at home, and build a nest-egg. Most staff were reluctant to stay long at the isolated Workhouse, 4 miles from the nearest station. Bessie's bicycle would help her travel home on her day off. The last cook had resigned in 1914, to become a nurse, and no replacements were found as war-work was better paid. Bessie pondered 'At least they should appreciate me. Father is just ashamed of me.'

From her first smell of the frowsy air, Bessie knew her new kitchen was badly managed. She almost gagged at the stench of dirty dish clothes, and greasy mops soaking in fetid grey sludge. Forcefully, Matron banged down a lid, and like a game of musical statues inmates and staff froze,

Mrs. Reason is now cook-in-charge." Two women lounged back on chairs, amidst the general busy kitchen pandemonium. Matron, eagle eyed, pointed them out "These women are your assistant cooks, Mrs. Hughes and Mrs. Nevard. Ladies, are you not working?"

Mrs. Hughes wriggled and gazed down, before standing slowly, with a weak smile "Welcome, Mrs. Reason."

Mrs. Nevard, who had applied for the cook's post, leaned back and crossed her arms, "It's our tea break." She stared long and accusingly. "Yes, we've heard all about Miss Reason." She looked at Bessie knowingly. Bessie felt Mrs. Nevard knew all about little Joan. She worried 'I can't escape from my past. Can I cope with managing these awful women, and all the responsibility? Still, I managed well in the army cook-house with Sergeant Field, and can show my true mettle here. I can cook for whole regiments.' Bessie stood up tall, and pulled back her shoulders determinedly.

Bessie lifted the stock-pot lid, full of slimy grey vegetables and bones, floating with unstrained, rancid fat. Bessie had prepared by reading The Workhouse Cookery Manual. "Matron, the pigs are going to feast today. This stock pan has to be thrown away immediately. Bones and vegetable peelings need to be put fresh in a new muslin net every day, and the net thrown out after 3 days, to avoid food poisoning." Matron smiled at Bessie's knowledge. Bessie turned to a lad sweeping "Please get help and take this out to the pigs. It is not fit for people to eat." He smiled, no-one had ever said 'please' to him before.

In the scullery, three thin girls, about twelve years old, scoured pots, sweat pouring down their faces. "What are your names?" asked Bessie kindly. No previous cook had ever bothered to talk to them. "Maisie, They call me 'Messy' 'cos of my wayward curls." Evelyn and Susan smiled eagerly back at this tall smiling woman, with glowing skin and shining hair. From that day Bessie rotated their duties, so they could learn more about kitchen life. Bessie also ensured their elementary reading and writing improved, by providing kitchen notebooks and pencils so they could record recipes. Bessie had told matron, she wanted to ensure the kitchen girls were fully trained for employment outside the workhouse. She also taught groups of girls to crochet to make dish cloths for the kitchen.

Bessie sorted through the pantry, and discovered tins of meat, dried prunes and currants, flour, sugar and empty preserving jars.

No jams, pickles or marmalade. The larder had one small basket of eggs; large cheese wedges, covered with mice droppings; uncovered pots of dripping and scraped fat, splattered with rodent foot prints; and traps full of rotting mice. Four large plum puddings lounged in the corner, crawling with maggots, Bessie smiled, as she pictured Flo saying "It will all help with the meat rations." Even Oliver Twist would not ask for more in this workhouse. Bessie had a lot to change, but was not afraid of hard-work. Immediately, she got staff to scrub down the shelves, and the kitchen lad to empty the mouse traps and reset them.

Bessie noticed hooks full of stained dirty aprons, ready to be worn again the next day. The clothing room was full of clean grey aprons. Bessie aware of the risk of Spanish Flu, threw all the dirty aprons in the laundry basket, and hung up clean ones ready for tomorrow. She deepened her voice and army-style instructed everyone to put dirty pinafores in the basket at the end of their shift. When they arrived, they must scrub their hands, and put on a clean apron. After supper, Bessie got staff to scrub down all the mouldy surfaces, and to sweep and wash down the floors. She overheard one panting woman "Young uppity bit, it won't last. Soon be back to the old ways."
Bessie retorted "High standards will be here as long as I am. Remember 'A new broom sweeps clean."

Matron took Bessie to the mother and new baby wing, where diets included extra milk, cheese and eggs. At the hungry sound of crying babies, Bessie felt her milk seeping out. She had only just finished weaning Joan, and bound her breasts with cloth, and was anxious Matron would spot a wet patch. Her past uncovered, she would be discharged in disgrace. Bessie felt angry at mothers, who chatted and seemed oblivious to their children. 'Oh, to be at home with Joan. Is she missing me?'

Bessie made significant changes in her few months as workhouse cook. Colourless beige food had previously dominated. Dried peas so old they were grey. Turnips, mangle-wurzels, swede, beet and potatoes mashed with fat, without gravy, or bread and cheese, were often the main meal: with the excuse of meatless days, following wartime shortages. Gruel, stewed mutton, hashed meat and butter beans, vegetable or beef broth had prevailed.

Bessie introduced a greater weekly variety, with pastry and steamed puddings included. Hotch-potch stew, popular in the army, was in the workhouse manual, and Bessie served this on her first day.

HOTCH-POTCH STEW
Ingredients per helping

5oz. raw beef free from bone - scraps or similar quality
1/4 oz. Flour
1/4 oz. Peas (whole or split)
3/4 oz. Scotch Barley
4 oz. Carrots or Turnips 4 oz. Cabbage
1oz. Onion Stock or water, sufficient to make 1pint.
Seasoning, Salt, Pepper, Herbs to taste.

METHOD:
Soak the peas overnight.
Scrape clean and cut the vegetables into small squares.
Scald the barley by pouring water over it, allow to stand for a few minutes, then throw the water away.
Add the meat, vegetables and herbs to the stock or water and simmer in a pan till the peas barley etc., are cooked.
Make the thickening by mixing the flour, pepper and salt with a little cold water.
Bring the meat and vegetables to a sharp boil, add the thickener and stir till it comes to the boil again, then simmer for half an hour.

The inmates were delighted to be given dishes such as Shepherd's Pie or sausages, and to have roast pork and potatoes, not boiled, on Bessie's first Sunday. (The workhouse had a piggery, but some Guardians had preferred produce sold, rather than pamper the inmates!) Apple sauce was added in late summer, when the crop was picked from the workhouse orchard. One arthritic old man cried with joy at his first taste of apple pie since entering the work-house ten years before. Everyone was meant to have an egg a week, and Bessie introduced fried eggs or bacon with Saturday breakfast. She made sure younger children had bread soldiers to dip in their boiled egg

Bessie visited the workhouse gardens early on, concerned at the absence of fresh fruit and vegetables on the menu. Spinach and peas were abundant, but unpicked. The large, ruddy faced, head gardener, was surprised to see Bessie, 'Never saw old cook. Said she'd not got time to prepare veg or fruit. Most goes to waste in the ground."

"Have you got workers to gather it regularly?" asked Bessie.

"I need more help for that. Enough to do with digging and planting, let alone picking."

Bessie looked directly at Mr. Evans, as she thought 'belligerent old bloke. He won't put in extra effort. Oh for Jim from the rectory garden.' Out loud she dealt her hand "It seems a shame for all your hard work to end up in the compost heap. I'll talk to Matron. See if more inmates can help. I'm sure we can work together in gathering the harvest. I'll get a team of women and children to help pick the peas. If you make sure the new potatoes and root veg are dug up. Let's talk about what crops are needed. Each Friday, we'll meet and agree on what needs picking for the next week." Mr. Evans knew he had met his match. Bessie arranged for teams of women and children to pick fruit and vegetables, instead of exercising in the barren high-walled exercise yard. Most enjoyed the change of routine and surroundings, especially the added bonus of gathering soft fruit. The infants loved sitting in the yard shelling and nibbling peas.

Bessie served stewed fruit and puddings, starting with the prolific rhubarb and gooseberry crops. Bowls of fresh strawberries, raspberries and cherries even produced a small upturn of the lips on some glum moulded faces. Bessie made fruit jellies for the invalids and children. She sterilised the preserving jars, and bottled fruit for the winter. In September, Bessie took a group of older children, including Maisie, Evelyn and Susan out gathering blackberries for an afternoon, with a picnic of egg sandwiches, currant buns, and cold tea. Maisie grinned, "Cor, Mrs. Reason, you've changed everything in the kitchen. Never had a picnic before. Phew, you're a breath of fresh air."

Life at the workhouse was repetitive, and a highlight was Sports Day in August for staff and inmates. Bessie was in charge of the food, and worked harder than ever, with a reduced staff. The local paper reported the day. For breakfast they had " tea, coffee, bread, butter and cakes....followed by Divine Service, conducted by the Workhouse Chaplain, where special hymns were sung. At midday dinner consisted of roast beef, ham, new potatoes, and fruit tarts, specially prepared for the occasion.' After clearing away, Bessie and the kitchen workers went to the field, where 'amusing events such as catch the grass pig, pillow fight, jumping and tilting with padded lance of soot and flour, sack race and tug of war." Bessie and her kitchen team beat the laundry team in the tug of war! They then rushed to prepare tea 'shrimps and bread and butter, followed by cake.' For the first time Bessie felt relaxed.

Bessie was praised loudly by the guardians for the dinner she provided for their September meeting. Best china and crockery were dug out of the storage boxes, and King Edward Coronation teaspoons produced by the Master for polishing. Bessie was reminded of the luxurious food she cooked at the Rectory, as she prepared the menu.

Guardians' dinner September 1919
*****

Beef consommé
with parsley garnish
Fillets of sole a la creme
Savoury Anchovies
****

Forequarter of Lamb with Mint sauce
Roast Grouse
Kidnapped kidney
******

Roast and mashed potatoes
Purée of carrots, French beans
******

Chocolate Soufflé
Queen of Puddings
Cheese straws

Bessie was annoyed that the amount spent on the Guardian's dinner would have fed the whole workhouse for a week. Most of the children had never tasted chocolate, and she had grated a whole block into the soufflé.

Bessie made a hidden protest by serving Invalid's Beef Tea, disguised as Beef Consommé with garnish, and smiled at the guardian's empty dishes. A small victory. The committee discussed their success in appointing Mrs. Reason as cook, with improved kitchen cleanliness and increased use of fresh vegetables and fruit. Concern was expressed at the profligate use of 300 eggs a week, but Matron pointed out that Mrs. Reason followed the Workhouse dietary manual, and now they had very little wastage. (When informed of this Bessie felt she was literally treading on eggshells!) Reverend Kensit-Norman joked that the pigs would be in danger of wasting away, with so little food wastage. Later, he visited Bessie in the kitchen to say he was pleased to have suggested her employment, in spite of her little problem. "You have made a good start, and not let me down. Keep up the good work, Bessie. We miss your well cooked meals in the rectory." Bessie stood open mouthed at the hypocrisy of the man who visited her home when Joan was tiny, to condemn her sinfulness. He even told Bessie to consider moving away, to stop shaming her poor father.

Every day Bessie thought about Joan. She kept Joan's photo secreted in her Bible. Her father had refused to take a photo of Bessie and Joan together. She worried she might mention Joan crawling, or saying her first words 'cat' and 'nana' (not 'mama') She would be discovered and sacked for immorality or deception. Although she made a good start, in the workhouse, Bessie resented seeing Joan only once a week. Home visits were going to be more difficult in the winter, with icy roads. It was already getting dark earlier in the evenings. Although Bessie's next visit home would be for their neighbours' funerals, she was still glad of an extra chance to see her daughter. Their time together was so precious. 'Roll on next week.'

See Postscript 3: Workhouse Jottings for more horrors of Tendring Workhouse

34: Bessie's Farewell

Baby Joan snuggled into the warm comfort of Bessie's breasts. Bessie was so happy to be home with her daughter, for a few short hours. Bessie felt her milk flow back, seeping into the bandages, tightly wrapped to restrict her motherhood. Joan smelt of rose petals and soap, after joyfully splashing in her sink bath. The first time Bessie had bathed her daughter for a month. Bessie longed to hold Joan tight for ever. Only a half day off each week from cooking in the workhouse. Bessie resented feeding some of the live-in mothers, who, although near their babies, were uncaring, deaf to their cries. She plonked porridge on those plates, and ignored their complaints and gossip.

Bessie belonged at home. A kettle sang on the glowing fire. Her father, George, was entrenched in his wooden arm chair, sorting his photo collection, pipe smoke drifting. He passed Bessie a photo, that he had taken, of Joan in her nana's arms, to take back to the workhouse. "Dad. Please take a picture of me with Joan, next sunny day. She is my daughter. We have no photographs together," begged Bessie. George glanced down, rearranging his photo collection not answering. He adored Joan, but still felt shamed by his daughter. He had risen from scaring crows in the fields as a lad to foreman of the Maltings, a proud man. Emily was knitting a striped hat from outgrown, unravelled jumpers, for her granddaughter, needles clicking at full speed. Elsie, Bessie's sister, smiled, and chattered about Joan trying to crawl to reach the kittens, "Oh I wish I'd been here, I miss Joan so much. I might not even see her first steps if I'm working." Geraniums bloomed, red on the window sill, the dresser full of freshly potted blackberry and apple jam, and green tomato chutney. Flo popped in from next door, blooming in mid pregnancy, and eager to catch up with her sister, before she returned to the workhouse. Warm chatter cradled them all.

Bessie bounced Joan on her knee "This is the way the old man rides, hobbledy hoy, and down into the ditch." Both laughed, Joan showing her first teeth. "Ring a ring of roses, a pocket full of posies, atishoo, atishoo, we all fall down." Mother and daughter giggled with joy and excitement. Bessie lifted up her wriggling daughter, safe in her strong arms, and walked round the kitchen, naming its treasures "Our dresser. Best china cups, striped egg cups, Nana's blue flowery jug, too special to use. Tasty jam. Look at the bottom drawer. Elsie and Ella slept there, when they were babies. Grandad is smoking his pipe. Smell the tobacco. A photo of nana, Flo, Millie, me your mummy, Elsie and Ella, five sisters altogether. We all made the rag rug. We each added one bird. Look at Ella's bluebird, made from her nightdress, flying away, my red breasted robin following, up into the clouds." Lulled by her mother's soft voice, Joan's head fell sleepily on her shoulder.

Wind rattled the windows, rain streamed down. A blast of cold air hit Bessie as her mother pushed open the door, back from the outside lavatory. Then Emily, small and thin as a sparrow, clicked the latch purposely, to defend the house from the outside devils. Bessie shivered. Spanish flu was creeping around, and had already snatched their neighbours, a kindly brother and sister, whose funeral they just attended. Two new inmates, at Tendring workhouse had suddenly died last week. Found cold in the infirmary after their first night. Bessie wanted to resign, to come home, but feared her father's disapproval, if she was a burden on the household. She needed to provide for Joan. "Bessie it's getting dark and stormy. I'm worried. Do you have to go back tonight?" begged her mother. Bessie gazed down at Joan, and felt tied to the chair, chained with love. She longed to stay. But, she would be fired. Her father looked reproachful, judgemental. He had found her employment, and Bessie would let him down again. She had already fallen from grace. Her mouth betrayed her, "I'm sorry, mum, I must get back or the inmates won't get their breakfast. I'd get the sack." Emily shivered.

Bessie gently handed Joan to Elsie "Look after her for me." She pulled her hat down, wound her red scarf round her neck, and wrapped herself in her waterproof cape. Hugged her mother and sisters, but father looked away. Bessie kissed her sleeping baby's downy head, one last time. Her bicycle lamp would not light. Her father leapt up to solve the problem and send his daughter away "Go carefully, love." Bessie hesitated as she opened the door, and gazed back into the golden warmth and love.

Bessie tucks her skirt up, climbs on her bike, rings the sad bell, and casts off into the storm. Cold river winds smack her face, she battles a path past lighted windows, and smoking chimneys. A dark night blanket covers her as she leaves the streets of Manningtree.

Her lamp only glimmers. Turning back home calls, but she keeps pedalling. She crawls cautiously uphill. Cold, breathless, lost, alone, tears and rain blurring her vision. Wind buffeted towards the hedge. Downhill will be easier.

Brakes not holding, skidding, screaming. Cottages rushing. Gate opening. A dark shadow leaping towards her, grabbing for her handle bars. 'Where did he come from, waiting silent and alone in the dark? Friend or foe?' Dark hat pulled down, over a bearded face, hard cold eyes, shouting loudly. Sudden stop. Flying. Owl calling. Branches attacking, scratching, clawing, hard trunk, stars falling.......

Newspaper Report Oct. 1919 cut out and kept first by Flo, then Elsie, all their lives

The Sad Cycling Fatality near Manningtree

The sad cycling accident at Horsley Cross which resulted in the death of Miss Bessie Emma Reason, aged 25, daughter of a foreman maltster at Messrs. Brooks and Sons, Mistley, and a cook at Tendring workhouse, created widespread regret and sympathy in the Manningtree district. The young woman was returning to Tendring at 9 o'clock on the 9th of October last, and in the darkness and the rain, it is thought with inefficient brakes on her cycle, she lost control going down the steep hill and collided with a pedestrian. Both fell and the deceased remained unconscious till her death next morning in the County Hospital at Colchester.

The Borough Coroner (Mr. H. Geoffrey Elwes) held the inquest -without a jury- at the hospital on Friday night, and the father, giving evidence of identification, said his daughter was allowed off on Wednesday night. She left Mistley about 8:45 pm to return

John Wood, a labourer, Gamekeepers Cottage, Horsley Cross, deposed that about 9 o'clock on the night of October 9th, he was walking home from Manningtree on the main road to Tendring and going down Ford Hill, Mistley. He was struck from behind

119

by a cycle and knocked down and a piece cut out of his right elbow. He had heard nothing of a bicycle approaching, but when he picked himself up he saw deceased lying in the road with a cycle at her side. She was unconscious and bleeding and he lifted her to the side of the road. It was as dark as pitch and raining. He went to Ford Farm, close by, and told the occupier what had happened. Mr. Holland returned with him, and on the gate, they carried the woman into the farmhouse, and a man coming along on a bicycle was asked to go for Dr. Bree. He ordered her removal to the hospital and she was taken there in the motorcar. Witness added that the hill where the accident occurred was pretty steep and very dark; there was no path by the side of the road. PC Bessley stated that when the deceased was brought to Mistley Police Station it was not known who she was. He telephoned to the county hospital to say the case was coming and asked the Sister to telephone if there were any marks on her linen to lead to identification.

Later in the night, the Sister telephoned to say that the person's linen was marked B.E. Reason, and as the result of enquiries he ascertained who the woman was. The officer added that he examined the road where the accident occurred, and noticed that the cycle wheel tracks went down the hill on the left side; then 15 to 20 yards from the spot where the collision occurred they zigzagged as though the rider had seen something and was unsure which way to go. He also examined the cycle and found the brakes defective. Deceased was probably travelling very fast at the time and she was a heavy woman. She had previously spoken to her mother about the brakes needing attention. The collision took place 9 feet from the left hand side of the road which at this point was 24 feet wide.

Dr. John McDonald, house surgeon at the hospital said the patient died at 6:10 am on Thursday without regaining consciousness. Death was the result of injuries: there was a small wound about 2 inches above the right ear and slight bruising over the stomach. He could detect no fracture of the skull without a post-mortem examination. The Coroner said he should find a verdict of accidental death and added an expression of deep sympathy with the relatives who are very highly respected in Mistley. He said Mr. Wood had acted with great kindness.

35: Saving Joan

Emily tugged the front door, swollen
from the river mists, not opened since
Bessie's funeral. A cold draught crawled
through the house. Emily stared at the
ill-matched couple, hovering on the top
step.

A tall skeletal dark woman, face etched with worry lines, eyes looking down, thin lipped, hair pulled back tightly under a small hat, and a blond man with dapper moustache, and direct gaze. "Good morning Mrs. Reason, we're William and Ellen Aldridge."

"I know who you are, Come in."

As Emily led them into the front room, Mrs. Aldridge brushed against Bessie's

photo, smiling, proud in her new uniform. William leapt to catch the falling reminder, and rehung Bessie's portrait. Emily retorted "Pity when you caused Bessie to fall in life, you didn't rescue her then. Sit down please." Ellen perched at one end of the black leather sofa, whilst William sat back. George filled the door frame, and William leapt up, hand outstretched but ignored.

George settled in his chair and stared. William started talking " We were so sorry about Bessie's accident." George rose to the bait, "Never know if it was an accident or grief, Bessie lost her joy of life, was shamed. She was a good, kind, loving girl. You deceived both her and your wife, a dishonest man. And I judged her too harshly. " The couple shifted awkwardly in their seats.

In the doorway, Elsie jiggled Joan up and down, and William gazed at his smiling round daughter. He reached out for Joan, who giggled and twisted the ends of his moustache. They gazed at one other in admiration. "Hello, little one, I'm your dad."

Emily watched William's wife, her face frozen, remote. William offered Joan to his wife to hold, but she lowered her eyes and retreated inside her shell. Emily would not let this icy woman bring up Bessie's daughter. "Do you have any children, Mrs. Aldridge?"

"No, it was not to be," she wiped a single tear away.

"Joan looks like her mother, smiling, blue eyed, apart from the blond hair." Emily stared directly at William. "Bessie was cheerful, a loving mother, but so missed Joan, when forced to cook at the workhouse to support her. Your husband sent no financial support." Emily paused and looked directly at William, who lowered his gaze.

Emily swallowed back her tears; "We have lost two of our beautiful daughters. We need to be sure Joan would be loved and cared for as much as we do." Then, Emily almost shouted, a strange sound for this kind woman. "You two are strangers, not used to children. Joan would be separated from a loving family."

Mrs. Aldridge scowled.

William gently kissed Joan. "I am her father. I would care for Joan."

George towered up. "Elsie take Joan into the other room." William kissed his daughter farewell. George dominated. "You ruined my daughter's life, you will not ruin my granddaughter's. You lack strength and constancy. Our family will love and care for Joan."

William and his wife stood. "Thank you for seeing us. I knew from Bessie you would be a hard nut to crack. I will send five shillings a month for Joan. Could I see her yearly?"

Silence echoed round the room. George opened the door to a harsh, whining, mournful river wind. Shoulders bent, the Aldridges began their long trek back to Manningtree Station. Flo, tall, aproned, and heavily pregnant, panting down the next-door passage, confronted them: "Bessie deserved much better, not a wolf in sheep's

Emily Field with her granddaughter Joan Aldridge Reason

clothing. You shattered our family. Killed the best sister ever. You will never steal my niece. Little Joan is loved by us all. Don't think you can kidnap her, and ruin her life as well."

As Mr. and Mrs. Aldridge retreated. Flo heard Mrs. Aldridge shout at her berated husband "I told you it would be useless. How could you drag me into that frightful family. They breed like rabbits. Are you sure that child is even yours? What ever were you thinking? You fool." William replied with silence.

William never saw his daughter again.

See Postscript 2 for
"Lost on Southern Railway: One Grandfather" -
My attempts to find William Aldridge

A family in mourning: Back row l to r Millie Flo Elsie
Front row George and Emily Reason

36: Dreamtime in Mistley Place Maze

Emily drifted into Dreamtime
from her fretful lonely sleep.

Mistley Place maze whispers,
murmurs to lost mourners,
and stirring graveyard ghosts.
Beech leaves skip, and scatter.
Concentric gusts wind Emily
tightly into a memory shroud.
Emily, once the gamekeeper's daughter,
housekeeper, replacement mother.
Home, a fairy tale cottage, secreted
in the woods, next to Poachers' Pond.
Dark, dangerous, icy in winter,
peacocks summoning the dead.
Evening creeping to the maze circles,
on Midsummer Night, true love seeking.
Lost and found, in joyful first kiss
at New Year, lamplit, mistletoe
hair entwined, dodged and hid
to find true love revealed
with an embrace for life.
Now Emily, the maltster's wife,
hunts two children lost in time.

Mistley Place maze, now war-torn,
overgrown, no magic paths,
blackberry branches brush-bound.
Emily beaten back,
in faded mourning black,
small, strong willed.
Concealed axe forced
out of foraging bag,

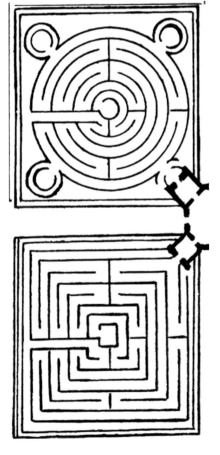

furiously chops.
Hands torn, face scratched, she
attacks the dark forest
to untangle the knot maze.
Anxious to remember,
to find her dead family
again, to make a new path,
to discover her lost past.

Mistley Place maze shadows
dart. A dead regiment
hide in the overgrown past.
Emily, statue-still, stares astounded
as William, her father laughs
in best gamekeeper's bowler.
Bear growls, plays, pounces as
his granddaughters maze-hide.
Arthur Sage trumpet calls,
just twenty,
tall, dead and handsome,
in blood red band-man's tunic.
One last echoing parade
after slaughter in Picardy.
Brother Ernie, too small,
glimpsed in the undergrowth,
rattles grain to lure back home
his escaped turkey cockerel.
Emily is stuck, uncomfortable.

Mistley Place maze middle
shrieks with silent laughter.
Bessie and Ella, two sisters
in berry-stained white aprons,
triumphant, first to reach
the concentric centre

127

Emily calls, held tight by
grasping branches, unable
to touch her beautiful daughters,
or pin up their escaping hair.
Her girls are never untidy.
Restrained from joining them,
by her bramble prison.

Mistley Place maze's playful ghosts
brush Emily's tear stained
cheeks. Spiral dance in
concentric rings, and escape
their maze. Hands joined,
William the jolly gamekeeper,
Arthur the wounded soldier,
Ernie the turkey keeper,
Bessie and Ella, sisters united
in a downhill country dance.
Through the distant lichgate,
to climb back into warm graves.
Emily torn between death and home,
longs to join in the dance,
pulled two ways at once.

Hesitant, Emily turns away,
stirs and slowly gets up,
and departs the Dreamtime,
to rebuild the maltster's family,
to mother tearful half-twin Elsie,
and to nana orphan baby Joan,
Weekly to visit her graveyard family
until she too joined
in the dance of time.

English Mazes (Weekly Telegraph18.01.1930)

The Maze at Mistley Place was planted by the Rev. C.F. Norman forty years ago.
The maze is perhaps, the finest of any such recently planted in England.The maze is in the form of six concentric circles whose outermost ring is at least thirty yards in diameter.It is made of beechwood and has for years been a very favourite resort with all the people in the neigbouring villages for picnics, festivities etc.,as its owner has always been most generous in lending it for such purposes, at which it provides no small part of the amusement for both children and growns.

Mazes and Labyrynths 1922, W.B.Matthews.

Another modern hedge-maze in the grounds of Mistley Place, the residence of E.M.Jackson M.A., who has kindl;y furnished the details....planted about fifty years ago, but unfortunately the choice of materials was not one of the most judicious, for while the major portion is Beech, young oaks were planted in the outer circle, and they have now grown up into large trees, now over-shadowing and ruining the neighbouring parts of the hedge so it is now difficult to complete the plan. Only the inner circle remains conplete.

(The maze was apparently replanted with holly in 1989 but seems to have disappeared.)

37: Queen of puddings

Bessie's Recipe 79

2oz. breadcrumbs
1/2 pint milk
2 eggs
the grated rind of a lemon
a little sugar
Add the grated rind of lemon to the crumbs,
pour on them the boiling milk, stir & leave til cold,
then add the yolks of eggs, & an oz. of butter and sugar to taste
Mix well & put into a buttered pie dish, & bake a pale brown.
put on jam & meringue & brown.

"Don't sit there, Elsie, it's Rose's chair," snapped Millie at her shrunken sister. Elsie was allowed to stay for a few days holiday with her sister at Kingsford Park, while the owners, the Digby family, were away. Millie realised Elsie was overawed by her first meal with the other servants. Wobbling her steaming soup bowl, Elsie half stood up to move, owl scanning the table for an empty space.

Rose smiled kindly "Don't worry, you're welcome to sit there." Elsie sank down on the hard chair, smiling nervously.

Annoyed by Elsie making her look petty, Millie stood her corner, "Elsie should have moved for you. She's only a visitor." Elsie's hand shook, as she tried to lift her spoon, to her clenched mouth, and pea green soup dribbled on the pristine white cloth. "Now look what you've done. For goodness sake, Elsie." In response, silent tears slid down Elsie's ashen cheeks.

The cook, Mrs. Thomas's sharpness shocked Millie. "I am surprised at your behaviour. You've upset your sister. Don't worry Elsie, we're usually all friendly here."

Millie scowled, she was normally Mrs. T's blue-eyed girl. Elsie's piercing look irritated her, *'She's playing the innocent.'*

Last October, at Bessie's funeral, she had held hands with Elsie, united in grief for their beloved older sister, who had mothered them both. Millie had tried hard to bond with Bessie's orphan baby Joan, but, when she tickled her feet too enthusiastically, Joan cried. Millie felt rejected as Joan reached out to her well-loved Auntie Elsie. At bedtime, Millie even tried brushing Elsie's hair, echoing Bessie's past care, but tugged at the knots. Elsie started weeping. Millie feeling useless and strangely sympathetic, surprised herself by inviting Elsie to stay at Kingsford Park.

At the servant's table, Millie felt nearly as out of place as her sister looked. How could she reconcile her treatment of Elsie, with her accepted amusing, competent and outspoken role. Millie attempted to regain approval through humour, and dropped her bread "What butter-fingers, and there was no butter on my bread." But the wry smiles lacked the normal energy and comfortable jollity of supper-time. "For tomorrow, I'll make Queen of Puddings, it's a favourite from my recipe book."
Mrs. T. smiled warmly at her assistant, "Millie has worked so hard writing up all her recipes. She is so keen." Millie watched Elsie's eyes opened saucer wide, shocked. A sharp kick from Millie stopped Elsie revealing the recipe book was carefully compiled by Bessie, only inherited by Millie.

 The next day, lemon and strawberry tastes wafted from the Queen of Puddings, swaddled under lightly browned meringue topping. Mrs. T. and Rose scraped their dishes and licked their spoons, "You are the Queen of Meringues, Millie."
But Elsie took one bite, then resisting the comforting taste, lay down her spoon, "Sorry Millie, it reminds me too much of Bessie, it was her best recipe."
Millie narrowed her lips, silently swearing, *'Outwitted again, Elsie always wins.'*

The sisters' love-hate relationship continued into old age. They wrote weekly with friendly news, but old rivalries surfaced face to face, with Millie constantly talking loudly over Elsie. Neither sister listened to the other, but comfortable in well-rehearsed roles, enjoyed twice yearly holidays together, and silently savoured each other's puddings.

38: Searching for Bessie

Joan was orphaned before her first birthday,
Bessie, her mother, dead in a cycling accident
Her family searched for Bessie in her daughter.
Some found connection and consolation,
others a strong-willed, outspoken child,
reluctant to hear reminders of her mother.

Grandad George grieved for Bessie.
Judged himself guilty of harsh rejection
of his jilted daughter, of bitter condemnation.
"Was he responsible for her lonely death?"
He heaped his guilty love on Joan, bereft.
Clasped her chubby infant hands,
took her weekly to the newsagents.
Joan stamped her feet and wept
crocodile tears, and begged for comics.
Grandad yielded, fearful of more distress.

Nana Emily cherished her grandchild,
Joan smiled, cuddled, adored her nana,
or scowled, feet planted grim and firm.
Nana, small, but strong-willed, always won,
with love, firm boundaries, and cunning.
Nana laced collars, stitched velvet coats.
Joan adored clothes and dressing up,
mirrored her lost mother's love of fashion.
Nana taught Joan to knit and sew perfectly.
Knitted patterns that entwined Emily and Bessie,
rewound with joy, mirrored by Nana and Joan.

Auntie Elsie stifled her grief at the loss
of her two closest sisters,
her twin Ella and then Bessie.
Focused her love on baby Joan.
Found Bessie's warm smile in her daughter.
Became an attentive second mother.
Bathed her niece, mashed her food.
Steadied Joan on her first wobbly steps.
Enjoyed her giggles at "Five Little Pigs."
Their mutual love strong and life-long

Auntie Flo inwardly blamed baby Joan
for Bessie's demise, but also adored her.
She searched for her sister in her niece.
Found her smiles, laughter, practicality,

but not Bessie reborn. Flo, ambivalent
veered from stern discipline to generous love
"Your tasty buns, are like Bessie's, your mother."
Joan scowled "Nana is my only real mother."
Apple of her grandparents' eyes, clever. But
Flo's son George toppled Joan's throne,
first grandson, named for his grandad.
Though many family photos of Flo's three children
included Joan, taller, dominant, smiling bright
"A cheerful cuckoo in the nest."

*Nana Emily and Joan with Flo and Nev's
son, George Sage*

39: Grandad George

When I was small, I learnt the women in my family ruled the world. My three great aunts were in charge, loving but controlling: Auntie Millie, an outspoken London pigeon, Auntie Flo, a wise observant owl, and Auntie Elsie, a busy house-Martin, quietly in control of her spotless nest. My mother Joan ruled the roost at home, made up the rules, which my dad and I obeyed, apart from small rebellions.

But there was another time, when the family was not matriarchal, but patriarchal, dominated by my great-grandfather, George Reason, 1858 -1935, a self made giant.

George Reason was born in poverty, the youngest of six children of Samuel Reason, agricultural labourer, and Sarah Jospall, who lived most of their lives in Chicken Lane, in the small hamlet of Little Bromley. Samuel and Sarah were unschooled, unable to sign their names on their wedding certificate, on 19th November 1837, resorting to crosses. Eliza, their oldest child was born in 1839, 19 years before George. All the older children were born in Little Bromley, but George was born after the family moved to Kihuana Farm in Lawford, three miles away. George went to school, an eager scholar, but started work at 12, scaring crows from the fields. Ambitious, he found work at the Maltings, Mistley, lodging with a family in Mistley Green by 1881. Mistley was a busy river port, with wealthy maltsters and barge captains residing in well established Georgian houses in the High Street. Whilst many large families lived in overcrowded houses, with open sewers running into the River Stour, and disease was prevalent

George was a keen church goer, encouraged by Rev.Charles Norman, who presented a bible to George in 1874, enshrined "from his affectionate minister." Later he became a church reader. George married Emily Field, the gamekeeper's daughter on April 15th 1891. Though he was not the complete paragon: their daughter Flo was born on October 28th 1891. A hard worker, George became foreman at Brookes Maltings on the riverside Walls, and moved with Emily to the Maltster's Cottage. George was an innovator, went to night-school, and learnt about the science of producing Malt. If only he had invented Marmite!

Malting could be dangerous. In November 1912 a Mistley maltster's labourer died from terrible injuries, when he put a belt on a pulley, when the engine was running at full speed. Fires often occurred from the drying process. On 28th July 1916 Free Rodwell Maltings, also in Mistley caught fire.

A good deal of valuable machinery and a large quality of malt and corn were destroyed. A daring act was performed by Jack Crisp, who when difficulty occurred in sending water on to the blazing roof, allowed himself to be lowered by a rope down the roof of an adjacent building, where he successfully directed a stream of water on the fire.

George on right with his team of Maltings workers

George was regarded as a good foreman, fair to his employees, aware of safety, with high production results. There were no accidents at Brook Maltings during his term as foreman.

George was a keen photographer, taking countless family photos, rarely allowing anyone else to use the camera. He appears in very few photos. An inventor, he built a stereoscope, which was well enough made to delight his great granddaughters in the 1950s. Ambitious, he bought a riverside family house, next to the Maltings, and then bought the next door houses for his daughters, Flo and Elsie, when they married.

Once, George was judged as less than perfect. He enjoyed a pint or more, and was angered by teetotallers' attempts to close local drinking houses. He was eventually prosecuted in 1909 for drinking in unlicensed premises

BEER AT A CLOSED INN
At Mistley, William Cook, an ex-publican, was summoned for selling beer, without a licence on April 29, and George Reason, a foreman maltster, and Cecil Balls, a maltster, were summoned for being found on unlicensed premises for illegally dealing in intoxicating liquor. Cook has been tenant of the Anchor of Hope, which until January 4 were licensed premises....No less than 126 gallons were consumed between January 4 and April 29 - Cook

137

said he had never sold a drop of beer since his license was taken away. The men came to his house as friends- the other two defendants declared they had never paid a penny for beer. The Bench, by a large majority, found the defendants guilty, and fined Cook £5 and 17/- costs, Reason and Balls 10/- and 4/- costs.
Chelmsford Chronicle 28 May 1909

Building a character from photos, historical records and memories creates a distorted reflection. In writing his story, from a 2020 feminist perspective, I feel both critical and admiring of great-grandad George as a self-made Victorian man. Family memories of George varied. His older daughters were raised by an ambitious despot, desiring high standards. George echoes Henry VIII, resenting he fathered no sons, announcing after each birth "not another old girl." He enjoyed control: "All joints on the table will be carved" as the girls rapidly removed their elbows. Bessie was severely judged for having a child out of wedlock. However his younger daughters, the twins Ella and Elsie, and his grandchildren adored their kindly giant of a grandfather. George and Emily guarded their tiny fragile twins carefully. When Ella developed tuberculosis of the spine at 12, George borrowed money for the first time to buy the latest rubber tyres wheelchair. After the sudden deaths of Ella in 1916 and Bessie in 1919, his grief seems to have made him kinder and more appreciative of his family.

In spite of his harsh treatment of Bessie, when she was pregnant. Elsie always cried with joy as she recounted the story how everyone was anxious how he would react, when Bessie bought Joan home; but were relieved when he stood from his wooden arm chair, and reached for the baby "Give the little mite to me, she must be freezing." But, in retrospect, George ordered Bessie to come back home after dark, not to shame the family! He did not greet Bessie. His words imply that Bessie was not capable of caring for her child. No photos exist of Bessie with Joan. He undermined his daughter, and stole parentage. George indulged Joan with comics and books, recognised her keen intelligence and strong will. He encouraged her to take the scholarship to go to Grammar School, and wanted her to fulfil her dream of teaching domestic science. Aware George was near retirement. Joan, knew the fees would be a struggle for her grandparents, and opted at 16, for a short secretarial course after her school certificate. Maybe to fulfil her own ambitions, she persuaded me into teaching,

"You are so good with your little cousins, and you will get school holidays, when you have children."

George appears less dictatorial after Ella and Bessie died within three years of each other. However, his tributes to his daughters varied, Ella buried in pomp and ceremony, carried in a black feathered horse drawn hearse, with a stone angel to mark her grave, whilst Bessie was buried at the edge of the graveyard in a gap between two footpaths, with no gravestone. George's paternalism continued even when his remaining daughters married. After saving to buy his home next to the Maltings, he bought the next door houses for Flo and Elsie and their husbands. Both Flo and Millie named their sons George, after their father. George was generous to the poor in his later life, small urchins would beg for a penny on the High Street corner, then run round the block and ask again; rewarded with another coin for their cheek.

In contrast to George, Emily was remembered by all her family as kind, loving and gentle. A perfect wife, mother and home maker.

When George died, he was buried next to Ella's grave, with Emily's plot reserved by his side. For George, proud memorials after death were important. George and his siblings had ensured their parents, Sarah and Samuel Reason, had the most prominent gravestones in the poor village of Little Bromley. Status continued in the afterlife.

40: Post-war Snapshots from Mistley Walls

In the autumn of 1919, Emily and George were still reeling in shock. Emily's dreams full of the departed. Every night Emily frantically jumped in the dream river to rescue her ghost daughters. Ella and Bessie were always swept away, or trapped under ice waves.

Away from the kitchen range, winter morning windows splintered into frozen ice stars, whilst cold draughts sneaked under the doors. Emily feared to take Joan outdoors as the deceptive Spanish Flu played hide and seek down the local passage-ways, and crept closer round cold corners. Emily had battled loss before, but felt diminished and drained. Joan looked up expectantly every time the back door opened. Then tightly cuddled her rag doll. and looked away with a disappointed face, whoever appeared, even her beloved Auntie Elsie. Emily felt Joan also waited for Bessie's bright smile to reappear.

However as a new decade arrived in 1920, life began to change for the family, and in Mistley. In the Spring of 1920, new patterns were established, which helped to splinter grief. Fortuitously named after his grandfather, baby George Neville Sage was born to Flo and Nev on March 4th 1920. George Reason was gleeful "My grandson, a boy at last". Small children distract from the dark corners of sorrow. Joan chatted loudly to outdo George's cries, and recapture Nana's full attention. Soon, Flo and Nev welcomed the birth of their daughters, Irene (Rene) in 1921 and Evelyn in 1923. Joan and her cousins were constant playmates, throughout their childhood.
It began to feel safer for George and Emily to loosen the reins on Elsie, even for her to leave home, but only next door!

Elsie became a house mother at Mistley Place, formerly part of the Norman Estate, now a preparatory boys school, run by Miss Eileen Jackson. (Elsie would later name her first daughter 'Eileen' in honour of Miss Jackson.) Elsie gave solace to small homesick boys with hot cocoa, and a bedtime story. Ex-pupils continued to write to Elsie for years, and later she grieved for many who died in World War Two.

Mistley thrived as a port for coal and grain imports and exports from the Maltings. Small ship building continued with Mistley's first steel built steamboat

Grandad and Nana with Joan and young George

launched in 1920. George bought a newspaper daily, and laughed loudly at a report headlined "SWOLLEN ANKLES" in 1923. A customs officer stopped a Chinese seaman, who tried to smuggle opium by wrapping it around his feet and ankles. After a month's hard labour, he was deported. Not a stone turned in Mistley without George's knowledge.

Major changes in road transport happened as motor vehicles dominated the roads, and horse driven vehicles began to disappear. Weekly,local newspapers reported speeding crimes and fatalities on unmarked cross roads.

L to R: Rene, George and Joan with nana Emily and grandad George in the middle

141

George enjoyed side car trips to local village pubs. Drinking and driving were unquestioned. Brooks' Maltings continued to thrive in protective paternalism, with George as foreman.

Annual Maltings charabanc outings to the seaside for families, and Christmas parties for employees children, were highlights of the year, alongside the strenuous daily grind.

Family outings by train to Dovercourt were enjoyed each year. In the photo Emily, Elsie and Flo are paddling with Evelyn, George and Joan, while Cousin Rene poses whilst digging. All the dresses are handmade in 1920s style.

Paddling in hats may have proved difficult once the wind blew! Grandad George could have taken the photo, unless he entrusted his camera to someone else, which seems unlikely.

The decade ended with a wedding: Elsie married Frank Seager on
May 4th 1929. Elsie's nieces were her bonneted bridesmaids.
Left to right, Joan, Evelyn and Rene Sage

Elsie and Frank Seager knew each other at school, but were very different characters. After the loss of Ella and Bessie, Elsie was anxious and serious. Emily and George had encouraged her not to start work until she had regained some of her old confidence, when she became 18. Elsie was practical, industrious, well dressed, with aspirations of gentility. She was a natural mother, becoming happier, as she mothered Bessie's Joan, and then house-mother at Mistley Place School. In the early 1920s Elsie wrote regularly to a 'well-spoken' butcher from the Midlands, who wanted to get married. But, Elsie was reluctant to leave the security of home in Mistley.

In contrast, Frank Seager was happy go lucky, and outward going, friendly towards everyone. He played in the local football team and the brass band, and enjoyed visiting the pub. Frank won his bride with good humour, and perseverance through a long relaxed courtship. Though Elsie had reservations on an early date, after Frank walked her home from the pub, but was so drunk that she then had to walk him home.

Elsie became more confident in Frank's company. A case of opposites attract.

George bought a house for the newly weds, a few steps away from home, next door to Flo and Nev. Three houses entwined for the next 50 years. Frank had not only married Elsie, but into her whole outspoken family.

Riverside Cottages, Silver Jubilee 1935

Flo and Nev Sage with children George, Evelyn and Rene - a photo that doesn't include Joan!

41: MIllie gets married

Millie, second from left, swimming with other servants in Scotland

Life as a cook in a large household suited Millie, she enjoyed the company of her fellow servants. Household staff were allowed to relax during holidays to Scotland, and gregarious Millie enjoyed being centre stage. She was capable and bossy, kitchen maids quickly felt the edge of her tongue if instructions were not followed exactly. An excellent cook, Millie happily catered for large dinners as well as continuous good daily fare.

Back in Mistley, Emily became increasingly anxious about her middle daughter Millie became quieter and distracted on her visits home, towards the end of the 1920s. On the night before Elsie and Frank's wedding, Millie was bitterly outspoken to Elsie "You could have done so much better. Less choosy as you get older?"

As Elsie ran from the kitchen in tears, Flo turned on Millie "Speak for yourself. You don't show much sign of marrying yet. You haven't mentioned anyone for years. You used to boast of a new conquest every time you came home." Millie banged down the rolling pin "Little do you know, I'm well looked after." She flounced upstairs.

Emily found Millie weeping on the bed. "You're unhappy, but you can't ruin Elsie's special day. What's wrong, my love?"

"I have been loved for years, but there's a problem. If I'm not careful, I'll end up a bitter old maid. I want to be married and have children. But it will never happen."

"Millie, please be careful. I don't want you hurt in the wrong relationship. Do you need to look elsewhere? You are no shrinking violet, try to see what's possible, rather than choose an unhappy false life. Be true to yourself. You don't want to look back in old age regretting what could have been. But for now, go and apologise to Elsie."

Millie marched into Elsie room. "I'm sorry, I should keep my big mouth shut. Maybe I'm a bit jealous." Elsie hugged Millie in surprise. Nobody in the family ever heard Millie apologise again.

Millie rarely visited Mistley in the next two years. She came home for Christmas 1930, and strangely seemed to delight in Elsie's baby, Eileen, born on November 9th. Bringing home, knitted matinee dresses in lemon, which Elsie accepted, but delighted in spotting one or two small mistakes. Millie had always rushed her knitting. Millie often held Eileen, and sang lullabies out of tune. Always generous, Millie bought an autograph book each for her nieces and nephew. Then blotted her copybook by telling Joan, who had proudly just won a scholarship to the girls' grammar school in Colchester "Good God girl, when are you going to stop growing, you're so plump and tall, you'll end up a giant" Millie made her point, and Joan stopped growing! She started as the tallest in her class, and when she left school at sixteen, was the next to shortest.

Evidence about Millie's late marriage

I am unsure where Millie worked in the 1920s, and wait eagerly for release of the 1921 census to see if she was still working at Kingsford Hall. By 1930 she was employed nearer to London.

Millie, when in service, was often driven by the chauffeur James Hepplethwaite Kemp, 30 years older than Millie, whose wife Lavinia died on November 5th 1930. In the postcard, from my cousin Val's glorious trunk of old family photos, Millie looks very relaxed and happy standing next to James. On the back is a message to their son

George, 'This is the car which Daddy used to drive, with Mummy and Daddy standing beside it. Love Mummy. June 1932."

Millie and James Kemp married in September 1931 in Holborn, much to the chagrin of James' eight adult children. Their son George was born on November 19th 1931, in Belfast. Why Millie would have travelled to Ireland for George's birth is strange, as there seems to be no previous connection?

We found a photo, taken on a visit to Mistley, I assumed Millie looked relaxed and triumphant as a mother.

However, by comparing photos, I realised this was taken 10 years earlier in 1921: Millie is holding Flo's son George. James Kemp died on 24th April 1936. Millie started work at Osram's lightbulb factory, and stayed there until she retired at 60. Millie inherited his home at 52 St Dunstans Road, Hammersmith. Probate records show that Neville Sage, Flo's husband, administered the will. According to family gossip, James' adult children were very angry about losing their family home. Millie was bad-mouthed in Hammersmith as a 'fortune hunter,' but seemed unconcerned: "Water off a duck's back."

Family legend says that George Kemp was raised by Flo and Neville Sage, after Millie was widowed, although this early photo shows George well settled in Mistley when only about 2 years old.

The postcard of Millie with her chauffeur husband, sent in June 1932, suggests George Kemp may already have been separated from his parents. Why they did not raise their infant son is difficult to understand, and gives rise to family speculation.

Grandad George welcomed baby George to the family. In spite of Millie's hasty marriage, he was proud of a second grandson named after him. Was he concerned about his new son-in-law being almost his age?

Millie spent all her holidays in Mistley, arriving on Christmas Eve with a large duck from the London Markets, and generous gifts for all. George followed his cousin George Sage to Colchester Grammar School, and then became a navy cadet at 16 years old.

George Kemp on left in Neville Sage's arms L-R Flo Sage, George Sage. Evelyn Sage, Joan Reason, George Reason, Rene Sage, Emily Reason. infant Eileen Seager, Frank and Elsie Seager

42: Joan meets Frank

In 1993 as Joan, my mother, lay in her sick bed, increasingly immobile with a brain tumour: she managed to escape by reflecting on the past. She smiled as she told me about her first meeting with Frank Watson, my father.

At Brantham tennis club dance, in 1938 Joan arrived in style, in a sleek polished car, driven by her friend Eileen's father, Fred Worth, the village hairdresser and newsagent. Joan, arriving with her good friends, Eileen Worth, and Jean Horlock, entered the village hall, chattering, laughing and boosted in confidence by each other. Frank leaving the bar with a tray of gin and tonics for his cousins, and a pint of bitter, lost his heart forever as he glanced across the room. In the middle of two dark haired girls, one with permed waved hair, powdered and lipsticked manicured face, the other tousle curled and laughing loudly, stood his dream woman: strawberry and cream perfection. Small, both natural and graceful, comfortably rounded, with blonde waved hair in a turquoise blue dress. Blue sympathetic eyes looked up into his face for just long enough to catch his gaze. Joan then turned to laugh with Jean, before glancing back and smiling directly at this new arrival; a stranger in the area. Frank froze in time, a statue. Then he remembered his cousins, delivered the drinks to Ruby and Pat with a quick pleasantry, before his eyes focused back on his ideal woman. He watched the trio of friends settle at the opposite side of the hall and, as the overture for the first dance played, decided to claim his bride.

Joan confident and smiling on the outside, chatted to hide her nerves. Last year, her heart and confidence had been broken at this dance. Charlie, her older boyfriend, had steered her outside after the waltz, and Joan fell into a loving kiss, but his hands started pulling her skirt up and his tongue filled up her mouth. After years of feeling different, illegitimate and then left an orphan as a baby, Joan was taking no risks. She would not be tarred with the same brush. No child of hers would be an outsider. She put her hands on Charlie's shoulders and pushed back "No, no further." Charlie's eyes hardened "What are you being choosey about? You were born the wrong side of the blanket. Your mother was no Virgin Mary." Joan was astounded by this change in personality, a wolf in sheep's clothing. Years of repressed anger burst out, and she punched hard. Charlie reeled back, retreated, and appeared at work at the factory on Monday with a black eye. Joan's new nickname was Boxer Reason.

Frank's confidence faded as he walked across the dance floor, then he noticed other eager partners moving towards the table with the three girls, and rushed. Joan smiled encouragingly, as this tall, wholesome stranger, with smiling eyes, skidded to a halt almost on her toes, and agreed to dance. Frank immediately felt protective, and in love with this small woman. As they danced she chatted naturally and Frank relaxed. He joked and made her laugh, comfortable in his arms. He even danced fairly well, legs a bit gangly, but perfect in hold. Joan felt sorry for him. His mother had recently died of pneumonia, after giving out gas masks in Derby after the Czech invasion. Frank felt he needed to get away from the grief. Only later Joan leant that Walter, his father, had turned to drink, and Frank could not stand to watch his deterioration. Frank had moved to live near his Aunt Mabel and family in Brantham, and to work at Long's the butchers in Manningtree High Street, just round the corner from Joan's family home opposite the river. Apart from politeness to his cousins, Joan and Frank enjoyed every dance together. A date at the local cinema was arranged for the next night.

My mother told the next part of the story with pride. When Frank arrived back at his lodgings, Mrs. Long, the butcher's wife, waiting up for her new lodger to come home, was astonished at Frank's enthusiastic reply to her question about the dance, "I've met the girl I'm going to marry."
"Who's that then?"
 "Joan Reason,"
"Oh, she's a very nice girl. You'll be happy"

The next evening, Frank was met by a cold blast from the river as he turned the corner to the Walls, He thought he had come to the wrong house as he climbed the three steps to the front door. All the windows were dark, but sparks and smoke from the chimney gave a glimmer of hope. He knocked and a dim light appeared in the hall. Joan's welcoming voice called out "Frank, come round the back. The bolts are stiff on this door," As the back door was flung wide, he knew he had arrived home. A waft of baked apples and Joan's fresh scent greeted him warmly. Frank already loved Joan, but was also overwhelmed by affection as a tiny, old woman hugged him kindly. Joan's nana, Emily, was delighted to meet this tall, kind faced, genuine man, after the two-faced suave Charlie. Joan almost had to pull Frank out of the kitchen, to go to the pictures, away from nana singing her praises. Frank was to become a regular visitor for Sunday lunch, as nana and Joan absorbed him into the family: even offered grandad's Windsor chair, empty since he died, at the head of the table. Emily recognised a good catch.

On the way to the cinema, Frank put his arm round Joan to protect her from the biting wind. Joan told me her story with delight. Her whole row of friends stopped watching the film, heads turned in unison to see Joan with a tall stranger. Whispers spread, "He's the new butcher from Derbyshire. Only just met last night." Their life journey was decided, and their engagement followed quickly, but life together would soon be disrupted by the war.

Frank carried this photo in his wallet throughout his life

43: Digesting another war

Joan Reason and Frank Watson celebrated their engagement in 1938, and enjoyed the summer, despite the shadow of impending war. Frank had learnt to drive and was able to take Joan on outings. The photo on Clacton Beach shows Nana Emily in best floral black dress, Joan's friend Jill, Joan, Frank and his cousin Ruby. All wear their smartest leisure wear for a visit to Cordys Restaurant for lunch, rather than paddling on the beach. The beaches are crowded unlike the war years to come, when they were mined and covered with barbed wire from the fear of invasion.

Everything and nothing changed at Riverside Cottages after the three households gathered around Flo and Nev's wireless on September 3rd 1939 to hear Chamberlain announce the nation was at war with Germany. They ruminated over the news with stout, cheese sandwiches and green tomato chutney. Blackout curtains were finished and hung in the next few days.

It could appear that routine life stopped during the war. Family photos are sparse from 1935 to 1945. George Reason's complex cameras stayed shuttered on the cupboard shelves, after his death in 1935. Regular summer outings by train to Dovercourt beach ceased after 1939. No family babies were born after Elsie's Valerie in October 1937, until a nest of post-war babies hatched out. The family was on a constant war footing, living through threats of invasion, with friends and relatives under attack at home and abroad. However, ongoing daily rituals helped to install calm, and deafen the increasing clamour of war. News was digested on weekday mornings when Emily, and her daughter's Elsie and Flo met daily, for a cup of tea and a cream cracker. Letters from Millie, working at Osram's lightbulb factory in London, and absent family were shared. This reassuring routine continued in the midst of ongoing drama.

Life was on a knife edge, from constant risk of bombing or invasion, plus anxiety about loved ones fighting abroad. Morning tea cups rattled with the latest gossip. Joan's close friend Elsie went to Buckingham Palace when her father, Edward Stannard, received a BEM medal from King George for stopping Manningtree railway bridge exploding. On June 10th 1940 Station-master Keeble spotted sparks from goods train had set the bridge alight, which had been mined ready for invasion. He ran to the signal box to stop the mail express from Peterborough due in two minutes. Guard Stannard from nearby Railway Cottages joined him, and they drew water in buckets of water from the River Stour. They burnt their hands as they dug out the bundles of dynamite and threw them into the river.

Moments of intensity or temporary joy burst the daily bubble. Frank, Joan's fiancée joined the Derbyshire Yeomanry, and whilst the regiment trained at Harleston, he came for regular Sunday lunches, with his old school friend, Archie Flixon, at Joan and Nana Emily's. The family celebrated Frank and Joan's wedding on January 20th 1940, and a year later cousin Rene Sage's wedding to Ron Tarbard. Neville Sage, now the family patriarch gave away his niece and daughter. Joan used her dressmaking skills to make bride and bridesmaid's dresses in powder blue chiffon velvet.

The newspaper reported *'A wedding of significant local interest of Joan Reason, the granddaughter of the late Mr. George Reason.... The bride's travelling dress was clover, with a navy blue coat and hat.'* Nothing like a war

Joan and Frank's wedding January 20th 1940. Left to Right: George Sage, best man, Frank Watson Joan Reason Rene Sage, bridesmaid, Neville Sage

would diminish Joan's sense of style. Guests shivered on chairs in the snow for photos, fingers and toes freezing, but still managed to smile. In spite of bombing, Auntie Millie's flat in Baron's Court was a regular free honeymoon venue! Auntie Millie worked at Osram's throughout the war, whilst George, her son, continued to be brought up by Flo and Nev.

Both brides continued to work, although pre-war, women had normally stayed at home once married. Joan was a secretary at Pages Garage in Colchester. Rene was a shorthand typist in Manningtree. Both were fire watchers, and Joan trained the local Girl's Brigade as a defence force in case of invasion. (third from right in the photo opposite). Both bridegrooms disappeared for most of the war, whilst their brides waited anxiously for news. Both fought in the Eighth Army in the North African desert, before joining the liberation of Italy, and the bloodbath at Monte Cassino in 1943

In a humorous wartime moment, Evelyn and Rene Sage and cousin Joan dress up in Neville Sage's old uniforms, stored in the attic which stretched acroass Riverside Cottages

155

44: Wartime honeymoons in Italy!

Montecassino towers resplendent above the Tuscan fields, rebuilt, monastic, ruling over a dried up, heat hazed plain of vineyards and wartime graveyards mingling in the distance. Grapes dry into sultanas on the vines. Fields with neat rowed plantings of slaughtered young men fossilise, never to grow again. Touring the abbey in the summer of 2007, our guide responds to my story of my dad, Frank Watson, liberating Montecassino. The guide diverts our coach of lunch-seeking Brits to visit the commemorative fields. As we descend into the past, all the chat about price of cappuccinos, and women forced to shuffle sideways, eyes averted, past urinating men to reach the toilet, dies out.

Silence screams, no birds sing, and lizards scamper in retreat from the approaching shadow-throwers. Dust, blessed by the sweet scent of crushed thyme, tickles dry throats and eyes. We had driven past the Polish graveyard, legions of tombs, and past other allies, Australians far from home, and stopped at the gate of one of the laundered British fields. Domino rows of tombs tessellate in never ending rows, forwards, backwards and diagonal. Order out of carnage. Well watered green English grass and rose bush borders. Now we wander in shock.

Coincidence or synchronicity or a guardian angel deposit me at a crossroads in time. The first row of tombs, all bear the same date in June 1943, and belong to the fallen of the Derbyshire Yeomanry. John Fieldhouse's inscription jumps up and shakes my roots. A young man of 22, who in his last years wearily ploughed through Tunisia with the Eighth Army. "So easily that grave could read Frank Watson, lance corporal. I wouldn't be here. Would the world be different? What would have happened to my mum, if no longer safe in a loving marriage? An orphan as a child and then a young widow. But, those bullets bore other names, strangers to me, comrades to my dad." Our family story was not buried in a distant grave. We can leave the day of judgement and savour pizza and citronella in a motorway cafe.

When he reminisced, Frank Watson viewed Italy through rose tinted glasses. Our photo album contained a photo of my dad and Archie Flixon, his mate, relaxed in shirt sleeves, with two young pigtailed girls in neat sailor-collared

dresses, and a small boy in Sunday best, the children of the family, where they were welcomed and billeted in the hills above Florence. After the summer battles of 1943, the troops savoured a sojourn of peaches, almonds, chestnut and sausage casserole, all drenched in the taste of the sun. A relief from corn beef and hard biscuits. For Frank, Italy cheered to welcome the exhausted soldiers far from home. Respite after desert tank battles, where the enemy swirled out of sandstorms, fired and disappeared. Dreams still haunted by a night of carnage in an orange grove, strewn with overripe putrid fruit, when the sleeping soldiers woke to a shot fired at a silent Arab slitting their comrade's throats. Frank retched at the smell of oranges for the rest of his life. Blood oranges were a bad omen for my dad.

Frank loved Italy, he felt at home. He repeated the story of how he became a hero in Italy countless times. If only I could hear him tell the tale once again, and not laugh at the repetition. 'Sent to reccy for fuel, We arrived at siesta in a hilltop village. We avoided the sleeping dogs sprawled in the road, and forced open the double doors of a dilapidated outbuilding. A large vat filled the space. Success. Not diesel, but sweet brandy.'

Once only, did Frank tell me, the horror story of his arrival in Italy. A memory shared as Alzheimer's broke down his protective brick wall against giving credence to hell on earth. "We arrived in the Bay of Salo, the troop carrier swayed in a thunderstorm, and the orders came to disembark. Smoke filled the air and tirades of gunfire mixed with the thunder, and ricocheted off the cliffs? We had to climb down a massive net on the side of the boat. We were hit by

157

a hail of machine gunfire, so many of my comrades lost their hold, screaming as they fell." The words dried up, and tears streamed down the old man's face. Dad's generation bottled up unimaginable horrors within stiff upper lips. His experiences are beyond my imagination, only stored in my head as an old silent black and white film, minus the sensory reality.

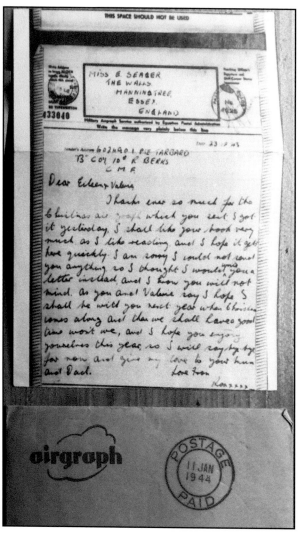

In contrast, Cousin Rene's bridegroom, Ron Tarbard's horrors continued well beyond the battle of Monte Cassino, where he was captured, and taken to a prisoner of war camp in Germany, in view of Colditz. Ron sent a letter to Elsie's daughters, after Christmas 1943, trying to be positive. However, when allied bombers struck, the guards set fire to haystacks and stood the prisoners in the chilling glow of the bonfire as human sacrifices, to attract the airplane bombardment away from the prison camp.

Ron was finally liberated in 1945, and retuned home, a skeletal shadow of his former self, weighing only 7 stone. He never spoke about his wartime experiences.

Dad's and Ron's stories were in sharp contrast to Lady Astor's view of the D-day Dodgers, parodied in song to the tune of Lilli Marlene: heartily sung in a concert for battle weary troops, by Lake Trasimeno, and later echoed on the long journey north to liberate Italy.

The D-Day Dodgers

We are the D-Day Dodgers in sunny Italy
Always drinking vino, always on the spree!
Eighth Army scroungers in their tanks
We live in Rome among the Yanks
We are the D-Day Dodgers in sunny Italy

We landed at Salerno, a holiday with pay
The Jerries turned the band out to help us on our way
Showed us the sights and gave us tea
We all had girls and the beer was free
We are the D-Day Dodgers in sunny Italy

Naples and Cassino were taken in our stride
We didn't go to fight there, we just went for the ride
Anzio and Sangro they're just names
We only went to look for dames
We are the D-Day Dodgers in sunny Italy

So listen Lady Astor, you think you know a lot
Standing on a platform and talking tommyrot
You're England's sweetheart and her pride
One great drawback your mouth's too bloody wide
That's from your D-Day Dodgers in sunny Italy.

Look around the mountains in the mud and rain
You'll see the scattered crosses, some that have no name
Heartbreak and toil and suffering gone
The boys who lay beneath them slumber on
They were the D-Day Dodgers who stayed in Italy

45: Grilled Knickers

"I've aired your knickers under the grill dear. It's a cold day. Would you like some toast?"

'Grilled knickers for breakfast!' Joan giggled and, exasperated, hugged Nana Emily, "Thanks Nana. I'm in a rush." Stuck in an upside-down childhood, Joan cared for her doolally nana; whilst Nana lived in the past and thought Joan was still a child, who needed looking after. Knitting jumpers, cuddles, warm cups of tea and buns ready as the school bus returned. A never ending childhood.

"Put on your school clothes dear." Confusion. Nana and Joan were both lost in time. Joan had last seen Frank two years ago. when he joined the desert rats in North Africa. No letters had arrived for the last three months. Joan, whilst smiling on the outside, was worried sick. Rubbing sleepy eyes, after a night fire watching on the church roof, Joan ran up the garden to the privy, then pulled on her coat and hat. Joan hugged nana, shrinking in her faded floral pinny, and grabbed topsy-turvey toast with marmalade on both sides.

Percy, the bus driver, practised his daily melody on the hooter in anticipation of Joan's warm smile, while Joan bolted breakfast, running down the passage: with a quick finger lick and glance at the sun dancing on the river. The morning bus to Colchester always waited for Joan.

Joan paraded along Crouch Street, proudly fashion conscious in rimmed hat, with powder-blue waisted coat, towards her ordered working life as secretary in Pages Garage. She planned to buy a matching skirt, as well as parachute silk to make replacement knickers, anticipating Harry's monthly gift of his elderly mother's unused clothing coupons: a thank you for help with bookkeeping.

Harry shuffled from one foot to another on the garage forecourt. "Tell me you haven't used this week's coupons. Have you? My mother died last Friday. They're illegal." Barred prison cells and black-market inquisitions seemed possible. Joan laughed nervously, oblivious to other threats hidden in the flotsam and jetsam of life's tidal surge: Frank was liberating Italy, under consistent fire in the battle of Montecassino, where many of his companions would remain forever in orderly graveyards, and air raid sirens wailed over her Mistley home, where nana was trying to light the fire with £5 notes.

Emily Reason

46: War's end

By 1944, everyone was on constant alert. Joan and Rene spent nights fire watching. Brothers in Law, Frank Seager and Neville Sage, continued to play trumpet and drum in the Church Brigade Band. Both joined the Home Guard, and caused mirth when the regiment was spotted marching down Colchester Rd. holding tree branches for camouflage. Frank's gun stood ready for action in the corner of the front room throughout the war. Frank was often on night duty spotting enemy planes. Once, all the family walked to Brantham to see bits of a shot down German plane. At home, daily patterns persisted. Elsie cleaned her windows every Friday morning, before six o'clock, when the factory day-shift passed by. Emily's daughters were a proud brood. Appearances mattered. Friday evening was bath night. Elsie ensured she heated fresh water on the range, to refill the tin tub for each person. Monday was washday, coppers boiled and mangles turned, with cold meat from Sunday's joint ready for a simple dinner

Millie Kemp, Emily Reason, and Joan Watson in the 1940s. Probably all the stylish dresses were made at home.

In spite of the nearby large plastics factory over the river at Brantham, few bombs fell locally. But in 1944, attacks intensified. A German fighter plane flew along the riverside and machine gunned near to children playing on the beach and paddling pool at Mistley. A bomb exploded one night, just over the road, knocking down the large elm trees and blowing a hole in the sewer pipe into the river. Flo and Nev's cellar filled with water, and floating sewage, which was pumped out. When Elsie woke Val in her cot, the next morning, her eyes had crossed in shock. After the bomb fell, Val needed glasses, which as a toddler, she constantly pulled off. Her reading was delayed, and hospital checks continued every 6 months until she was 11. Elsie had anxious migraines most Sundays for the rest of her life. Traumatised as a child by the deaths of her closest sisters, plus the added anxiety from two wars. Fear grew as flying bombs, doodle-bugs, regularly followed the river banks, towards inland targets. Everyone listened apprehensively for the clamouring engine noise to stop: warning that the bomb would explode, after a few seconds of loud silence. Frank, holding his terrified daughters' hands,

often took them outside to watch the dark clamouring shadows of the flying-bombs, pass along the wall. Meanwhile local children continued to swim in the river avoiding any floating sewage.

VE Day band parades, recycling of Coronation bunting, and a street party in Manningtree High Street signalled a complete life change for the family. Ron was released from prison camp. Frank returned from the front and resumed work at Turner Village mental hospital. Both Joan and Frank worked in Colchester and in 1946 moved to a downstairs flat, in Creffield Rd.

Two years later, their daughter Sheila was born. For years, Joan referred to Mistley as home, her closest friends and family lived there. She missed their daily support, especially when she stopped work, and was at home for my first five years. Joan thrived on company. Every Sunday for twenty years we returned to Mistley for family tea. New rituals had started.

Before the war, Frank had been a butcher at Long's in Manningtree. He enjoyed serving customers, but found butchery of fresh carcasses increasingly stomach-churning. An advert for a post as a trade-nurse at Turner Village in 1939. provided a welcome change of direction. He became a benign jack of all trades, a positive encourager. Declaration of war provided a jolt, a major unsought detour into enlistment, back to his roots to join the Derbyshire yeomanry. Desert battles in the Eighth Army in North Africa, followed by the liberation of Italy, provided a surfeit of carnage. Frank left butchery for healing, and in 1945 returned to Turner Village as a trainee mental health nurse. But he found himself in a 'madhouse'. Psychopaths from Broadmoor Hospital had been rehoused during the war, and Frank became part prison guard in an insecure institution. Eventually, Frank was hospitalised, after a maniacal patient escaped, intending to find and kill his mother. Frank joined the manhunt with police and nurses running in long wavering line, across misty fields towards the station. He won the race! After rugby tackling the escapee, Frank pinned him down, whilst the patient kicked out and broke six of dad's ribs. Eventually enough police arrived to carry away one aggressive patient in a straight jacket, and one wounded healer, on a stretcher. Frank was nursed in Essex County Hospital, where on recovery, he metamorphosed into a nurse on basic training, to become a certified mental health nurse. Sister Duggan used to training young female school-leavers saw no reason to change her methods for returning soldiers, but white jackets lacked the opportunity for enforcing uniform regulations that nurses starched caps and aprons offered. Frank respected Sister D and internalised her ideals for best patient care, high standards, fairness and hard work.

Back at Turner Village, Frank's efforts were rewarded by work with the 'high grades' and quick promotion to charge nurse on Villa One for the next 30 years. Routine provided a haven after the battles of previous years.

Nana Emily lived long enough to hold her first great grandchild, Janet born to Rene and Ron Tarbard in 1946. Emily, now very confused and weak, was looked after by Flo and Elsie, who supported her in turn, as she drifted in and out of sleep. On the morning of November 15th 1946, the two sisters were thoroughly cleaning Emily's spotless house, whilst Val sat by her grandmother's bedside. Intently Val held up transparent pictures in a story book to view the rainbow colours. At 11 o'clock, Emily's daughters came upstairs, with three cups of tea and cream crackers. Flo whispered "Mother has started her big sleep." Elsie opened the window, of the room, where Emily once gave birth to her daughters, for her soul to depart. Both gentle and determined, Emily had lovingly mothered three generations, for 65 out of her 78 years.

First her younger siblings, then her five daughters and then her granddaughter Joan, who had only just left home.

Rene and Ron, with baby Janet, moved into Emily and George's empty home, next door to Flo and Nev's, in continued family support and proximity. I was born in February 1948, and the family celebrated with small winning bets on 'Sheila's Cottage' an outsider in the Grand National.

Rene was expecting her second child, when Nev suddenly died on April 15th 1948, with a massive haemorrhage. Flo's hair turned white overnight. Their daughter Rene, pregnant and shocked, was covered in a rash until baby Ann was safely born, terrified by an old wives' tale, that if a pregnant woman saw a dead body, her unborn child would die. In spite of reassurance from a midwife, and the arrival of the National Health, old beliefs dominated. Flo was forced to live proudly and frugally on a small widow's pension for three

Rene and Ron Tabard with daughters Janet and Ann

years until she was old enough for a state pension. As a child, I was amazed that Auntie Flo spread butter or jam on her bread, but not both. She avowed that jam hid the taste of butter. Generosity continued as she hooked a rag rug for every new baby in the family. Birthdays and holidays were celebrated. George Kemp, enlisted in the navy at 15, came home for his 21st party in 1952. My amazed memory is George, only wearing pants sitting in the laundry basket, with two sailors drawing on his chest with lipstick. My mother quickly tucked me up in bed, next door at Auntie Elsie's.

47: Needles and pins

Needles and Pins.
Bessie, Millie, Elsie, Ella and Flo,
Emily taught all her daughters to sew.
Fabric from the haberdashers,
colour matched, fit for purpose,
wrapped in brown paper,
adorned with a string bow.
Packet of pins given for change.
Paper pattern jigsawed,
pinned, tucked, and cut,
scrimped, no waste.
Scraps hooked into rag rugs.
Careful savers all.
Hobble skirts, pinafores for school,
aprons, dresses for under cooks.

See a pin, let it lie,
all the day was not good luck.
Elsie's twin, Ella, lost to meningitis.
Her last wish a black feathered
horse for her funeral
'Not a new fangled motor car.'
Extra hem on Elsie's mourning
borrowed from Ella's unwanted
last black schoolday's skirt.
Nothing ever wasted.

Needles and pins.
See a pin, pick it up.
Emily swept away her tears
"If I cry, I'll never stop".
Bessie lost next,
stolen by a bicycle crash,

night riding, rushing to cook
breakfast in the workhouse.
Emily cocooned orphan Joan;
confident dressmaker, recycled
Bessie's best blue velvet skirt.
Paper pattern laid, pinned cut,
enough for an infant's hat and coat,
lace and ribbon trimmed for Joan.
Feet firmly planted, stockings knitted,
photo staring for a hundred years.
Waste not, want not.
See a pin, pick it up.

Needles and pins.
Emily taught Joan how to sew.
new sewing machine whirring,
first zip fitted, no mistakes.
Later, a busy, busty, school secretary,
pattern laid, Joan copied, cut,
no waste, checked dungarees
three dresses, ruched
Peter Pan collars, buttons
hand covered, perfect fit.
Bluebell holding, laughing,
her daughter Sheila and friends,
photo smiling for sixty years.
See a pin, pick it up,
Pass it to a new generation.

*In homemade dungarees to keep
my dress clean*

L to R friends Yvonne and Linda Piper with Sheila

48: Past and present in Flo's house

Three, weekly whitened steps,
descended only for funerals,
lead from the riverside to the front door,
never climbed, door closed, firmly bolted.
Great Auntie Flo lives in this house.

Left to right; Great aunties Millie, Elsie and Flo
Next to the old pump and outhouse, in the shadow of Brooks Maltings

Skip up the side passage.
Back gate latch click.
Back door never locked. Knock.
Opening, warm welcome cuddle,
strong arms comfort, bosom hug.
Long white old hair pinned up, topped
with a bright yellow badger stripe

of magical unfaded youthful hair:
once a child now wrapped in old wisdom.
Eagle eyes scan, laughter lines wrinkle.
Free to be me here, a child, to play
in Auntie Flo's humorous house.

Flo settles alert in her wooden chair.
Kettle steams, teapot ready,
iron range top clashes open.
coal glowing.
Family tea gossip,
all talk, rarely listen.
Best bird cups soar up and plunge down,
futures revealed in motley leaves.
Teenage cousins dance the twist
pulling towels hip to hip.
Flo, our family matriarch, oversees
a repeating Sunday afternoon
life dance in her riverside house.

Never-ending generations chatter.
Secure on my small wooden stool,
I play with the book shelf treasures:
card pack, spinning top, bagatelle,
Enamel tin of old buttons reveals
giants, babies, glass jewels, gems,
soft baby buttons, bridal pearls,
military brass, and mourning black.
All of life hidden in a tin
in Auntie Flo's play house.

Auntie Flo stands with purpose,
advances on a frantic buzzing
wasp, window trapped. With
her bare finger squashes her intruder,

and throws it out of her safe house.
Flo tells tales of her servant life,
lost on her first home leave,
climbing a stile to find her way home.
"You rock backwards and forwards
like your nana. Such a sad loss,
Bessie, my dear sister." Memories:
photos of Nev, her handsome husband,
died soon after I was born.
Smiling girls draped in long locks,
a meadow row of blond flowers.
now our permed sensible mothers.
Past lives in the present,
never ending stories in Flo's house.

Left to Right, Evelyn and George Sage, cousin Joan Reason, Rene Sage

Fireside cupboard treasures.
"Stamps for your collection, penny reds,
Indian rulers torn from Nev's envelopes,"
enfolding love letters from
a long-ago military drummer.
Postcard from Bessie in 1917,
safely back at Aldershot barracks,
a slave in the wartime cookhouse,
to sister Flo, 79 Cromwell Road,

a cook for the well-off gentry
"So posh, they wore two hats on Sunday."
Lost lives linger in Flo's house.

Front room cupboard hidden behind
the black horse-hair escaping sofa.
A locked trapdoor to the cellar, bombed
and river-sewage flooded in the war.
Cupboard shelves groaning
bursting with rags and old clothes,
sorted and graded: funeral dresses,
Holey lisle stockings, worn pinnies,
petticoats, twice knitted jumpers.
Tatter cut, hooked into rag rugs by Flo,
a gift for every new family baby.
Fantastic coloured animal decorated,
stories streaming from Flo's house.

Coffin table in the front room, seats
twenty six for Christmas tea:
celery crunch, cider punch.
Also Auntie Flo's last resting place,
after waiting for her big sleep.
Laid out by her sister Elsie
daughters Evelyn and Rene.

Departing out of the front door,
unbolted with 3 in 1 oil and ceremony
Down those three whitened steps,
along the riverside, to join
Nev, Bessie, Ella, mother and father
in Mistley Church graveyard,
with space lined up for more.
A funereal kitchen feast,
prepared by family, all chattering.
Calendar updated, fire blazing,

kettle singing, strained tea.
What's forecast in the leaves?
A houseful remembering Auntie Flo.

49: My Sunday afternoon harbour

River winds buffet, blow our
hair backwards, tease our eyes.
Until
we turn a corner, climb up
a steep cinder passageway,
through lichen weathered red brick cliffs,
to my Auntie Elsie's 'lighthouse.'
Sparkling windows, polished weekly
mirror our glowing faces.
Elsie in pinny, over Sunday best,
small, round glasses, rose scent.
Warm smile in front door welcome,
encompassing hug, our haven.

Well polished table gleams.
Orange and ginger dahlias
dance with amber fire flames.
Apple pies and biscuits baking.

But, one Sunday,
when river damp creeps,
smoke seeps and curls
from the damp coal fire.
Uncle Frank stretches newspaper
across the insipid fire,
draws embers into flickers,
flaring upwards into chimney roar.
Order restored, Frank
vanishes to the outhouse,
scrubs soot off allotment celery,
peels ditch-dug horseradish.
Safe from the Sunday invasion

of matriarchal family women,
in his harbour from the storm

Kettle whistles on the daily
blackened kitchen range.
Bubbling brown brew, in
Sunday best china cups.
Laughter, chatter, gossip
in well rehearsed tunes,
sing-song in local Mistley lilt.
A tape-recorder hidden once
"Oh, who's that talking so much?"
Mirth roars, sides split,
"Why, you of course, cousin Rene."
A familiar safe mooring.

Over 50 merged married years,
Uncle Frank's tomatoes abound,
sweet peas bloom, beans climb.
A new bathroom built, squeezed
in half the small, old kitchen.
No more outside toilet trips,
no boiled water for tin baths.
A new electric cooker, polished daily,
a fridge and even a spin drier.
All safe inside this ship-shape house.

Careful.
Death is lurking outside.
Grief stole Elsie's childhood,
took sisters Ella and Bessie;
then shattered old age as
Grandson Roy's car crashed.
Comfort others, bury the pain.
Order, routine, ever busy,
scrub, shine, keep germs at bay.

Find solace in family. Smile.
Joy of fresh picked flowers.
Cook Christmas puddings,
silver coins hidden inside.
Treasure the children.
Pull the curtains against the storm.

*Elsie and Frank's Golden Wedding,
bridesmaids left to right Rene, Evelyn and Joan*

A Golden Wedding celebrated,
bridesmaids now pensioners.
Generations of love,
gathered in Elsie and Frank's
refuge from the rising tide.

Times change.
Rheumatism racked Uncle Frank,
"I've got the screws today,
I'll end up in the spike.
Everyone I know is there."
"Don't be silly, Frank. I'm here.
You're not going anywhere."
Brush age into the corners.

Death stole Uncle Frank.
Elsie scrubbed, swept and polished,
greeted great grandchildren,
knitted perfect baby clothes. Even
extinguished an electric blanket fire,
before the fire engine arrived.
But repeated the same sentences,
fell down the stairs at ninety.
In hospital, anaesthetic confused,
demanded to see her new baby.
A miracle birth!
Quietly accepted her big sleep
to find her lost family
in a new retreat from the storm.

50: My dad works at the funny farm

"Don't wave, pretend we don't know your daddy."

'What was happening?'

Mum and I sat proud and untouchable in the 3/6d. seats, whilst my dad, Frank, helped a group of his lads down to the cheap seats at the front of the Saturday afternoon pictures. My dad, a mental-health charge-nurse, in suit and tie, stood out a head higher than these men, who were called 'boys,' 'mental patients' treated forever as children: all wearing trousers that ended mid-calf and jumpers too short in the sleeves. Some of the infantilised Peter Pan boys happily waved to all of us awaiting the B feature in the twilight cinema. The usherette shone a torch to guide the lost group. Some 'high grades' led others by the hand, one lost boy turned in semi- circles, making bird noises, until my dad gently guided him towards the row of seats, Surrounding seats were left in isolation by later arrivals. A segregated group judged by society as weird, outsiders, 'retarded', 'nutcases'.

I was perplexed by my mother's reaction. Now, I understand her fear of the unknown other, mixed with a desire to be not seen as of limited means, still fearful of the workhouse and associated institutions. A desire to be accepted. As a child, Joan had felt different, ashamed of being illegitimate and angry with her mother for dying, when she was a baby. Now, she would not be tainted by association. Her friend's were better off and had the money to achieve middle-class aspirations. My mother was a school secretary, proud of her role, and of her husband's recent promotion, as long as his work was separate from home. Joan sat in the cinema, modelling a turquoise feather hat, 1950's navy flared coat, carefully brushed, and matching navy leather shoes, gloves, and handbag, all first day of sale bargains. My coat was dark cherry, with velvet collar and matching beret. In the interval, a large hankie covered my coat, in case I spilt the ice cream tub, whilst my mum carefully enjoyed a choc-ice. We waited for the usherette to finish serving dad's group, and to move back up the aisle before getting our ice creams.

From birth, I was aware my dad had a very important job, at the 'funny farm' looking after men who found it hard to grow-up. Political correctness was unknown in the 1950's, but Turner Village was founded on humane ideals, where patients were encouraged to develop life skills. Laughter always followed the story about when my dad proudly took a photo of me as a newborn to work, and overheard one of the inmates "Mr. Watson is showing everyone a photo of a bald-headed little monkey." I could see nothing humorous, obviously I didn't fit, 'I was weird, Would I live in the funny-farm, when I grew up?'

Work and home were separated. My dad was my hero, who towered above everyone else and cared for his lost boys. Bicycle clips were the signal for his disappearance to work, replaced in later years by a helmet for his moped. On days off, Frank took me out as a toddler, leaving me in the pushchair tied to the railings of the Sun Pub in Lexden, (normal for the times, not viewed as child-neglect), while he swallowed a quick half. When off-duty, he supported Colchester United every home game for life. Frank was a keen gardener, straight rows of vegetables, onions, tomatoes, carrots, the first in the family to dig up early new potatoes or pick his runner beans. He was a keen canasta player, reader of war and detective novels, a self educated man devouring correspondence courses, on Prehistoric man, geology and weather. Comics were read to me with love. Frank weekly bought me Robin then Swift, and once, even tried to introduce me to The Eagle one week but teasing by Joan that he wanted to read a boys comic himself reinforced my love for Girl and Bunty. Years of comic sharing ended by stereotyping. Later my enthusiasm for Biggles in the Gobi Desert, saving the whole world, provided a temporary sharing of books.

Daily patterns differed from our neighbours. Night duty reared its ugly head, when my mother's fear of the dark would mean my removal to the z-bed in her room, with the bedroom door bolted and a chair propped against the door to ward off all intruders. Shift working from 6am to 2pm or from 1.30pm to 9.30pm created problems and opportunities. Dad tried cooking when home in the afternoon, and created chicken curry with apples and sultanas, superb apple pies, and coffee and walnut cakes. A limited

179

repertoire but an exciting change. Joan was always the main cook, but Frank was a 'new man' unfettered by stereotyping.

Christmas dinner was dependent on shifts, early at 11.30 for the afternoon shift, or eaten at teatime after the morning shift. A game of snakes and ladders or ludo, making paper chains, and pulling a cracker provided safe routines and limited magic. When I was ten, I even spent the day happily engrossed in my new Unstead Children's History, escape into the past with Roman invaders, Florence Nightingale, and into Victorian slums; joy for an only child. In the evening, Valli and John, our Latvian neighbours came in for nibbles and drinks, and to watch the Billy Cotton Band-show, eventually joined by my hard-working dad. I resented dad's boys, having fun, taking precedence, and stealing him at Christmas. Every third year my dad had a day-off. Then, there was enjoyment, excitement, when we could join all the family at Manningtree, with at least 20 relatives laughing at party-games, pass the ring on the string, charades, pass the balloon, wink and McGinty's dead. Real Christmas.

Frank never escaped the world of mental hospitals, transforming in old age from carer to a patient, lost in Alzheimer's. He often believed he was at work, grabbing the staff nurse's notes, "I never seem to have a day off. I'm at work all the time."

51: 'Tis the season to be merry

Christmas is coming.
Where is Christmas Past?
Memory splinters:
a slow motor cycle, sidecar squashed,
a pyramid of mum, cousin Pauline, presents and me,
Ice white, purple cold. Sidelong glances
at hoar frost fields, skeleton trees.
Shivers, frozen breathe
on our way to Manningtree,
Back to Christmas Past.

Christmas is coming
What is Christmas past?
Woken by frantic shouts,
snuggled in soft down mattress,
Squawk,
"Catch the chicken it's running around, headless."
Great aunts feather pluck, gut, stuff,
potato peel, chop, stir, chat, and laugh.
Under the kitchen table,
one overwhelmed child
watches the busy dance of feet, and
hides from well rehearsed Christmas Past.

Christmas is coming,
When is Christmas Past?
Family evening games:
find the curtain ring
pushed round a circular string.
 Great aunties murdered by a wink,
playing Mrs. McGinty's dead
Oranges passed chin to chin
by runny nose cousins, and stubble uncles.

Pickled onions and tobacco breath. Fun?
Warm spiced mince pies, celery
sticks, much scrubbed but soot gritty.
Creme du Menthe, egg-nog,
sherry and foaming beer, and laughter shrieks.
A lost child in Christmas Past,

Christmas is coming
Who is Christmas Past?
Candles smoke and glisten after dinner
amidst green ivy and holly.
Nuts cracked and oranges peeled.
Great Auntie Elsie softly sings
'The Mistletoe Bough' and weeps for
long lost sisters Ella and Bessie,
and all the other ghost guests.
"A toast to absent friends."
Family comfort in Christmas Past.

Christmas Past is when
my dad jauntily plays the spoons,
recites 'Albert and the Lion'.
My mum's smile freezes to
his resonant song, the 'Foggy, foggy dew,'
A reminder of her mother, Bessie's sin,
unmarried birth, and then death
flying away, over her handlebars
on a dark, winter's eve,
leaving her daughter Joan,
abandoned, not alone.
Nana and grandad, and Aunties
Elsie, Millie and Flo wrapped Joan up,
A lost orphan swaddled by family love.

Christmas, when past echoes into present,
and onwards to the future.
'Tis the season to be merry.'
.

Three generations:Sheila, Joan and Jenny at Manningtree
Christmas 1987

52: Great Auntie Millie

Great Auntie Millie's plentiful bosoms shook when she laughed. She was a frequent visitor to Colchester for short breaks, but always lived to her own maxim: "fish and visitors stink after three days". As a child, I would have loved her to stay forever. She told Punch and Judy stories with rolling laughter, of horrific beatings with sausages, and Judy and the baby throwing Punch away. She taught me Clock Patience, and told stories of her life as a cook in service, about living in London, with streets paved with gold, but beware of the dog muck. Her opinions were forceful "You don't want to sit on that wet grass, you'll end up with rheumatics like me. Look at my shoes, they're specially made for my ankles".

How silly, I was just a child, who would never be old with rheumatics. I laughed and finished her daisy-chain necklace, which she wore with pride. "Don't go picking those dandelions, you'll wet the bed". Auntie Millie supported me in my attempts to stand up for myself, against my strong minded mother. "I'll lay the table Joan, let the girl play her records".

Millie told Joan how to string and cut runner beans. "Auntie Millie we both learnt the same method from nana, I know how to cook just as well as you." Millie would not be beaten. "I'll make Queen of Puddings, if you like." Joan was unable to resist this offer or match Millie's meringues. We gobbled them up for lunch with joy, and then for tea relished Joan's well risen, icing dusted Victoria Sponge.

Millie forthrightly demanded "I enjoyed that. How did you manage that, girl?"

Joan's ample breasts swelled with pride "I use three eggs and beat for an extra five minutes when it's creamed." Triumph.

"Any fool can bake a cake with three eggs. Good job rationing's finished". Millie's chest thrust victorious, as she enjoyed a second slice, while Joan choked on a crumb.

My mother breezed a sigh of relief when Millie squeezed her in a suffocating goodbye embrace. Both women were matriarchs from the same nest, where Emily had raised them with kindness, determination, and ambition. Aunt and niece were both convinced of their opinions, wisdom, and superiority. After doubting myself in younger years, I inherited the matriarchal gene. None of our family are ever wrong.

Great Auntie Millie was a Londoner, who kept secrets. She lived at 52 St Dunstans Road, Hammersmith, an upstairs flat in a large Edwardian house, and rented out the downstairs. She inherited the house from her husband, much to the resentment of his grown up children. Millie, a super proud mother, boasted nonstop about her son, George, a lieutenant commander in the Navy. But his birth was shrouded with mystery, a source of family speculation among younger generations. Why was George born in Ireland, with no previous family connections? Why was Millie, just 33, attracted to a man of 63? Millie went every year on holiday to servant friends, living in Chipping Camden, but kept George a secret and never mentioned her son over the next 50 years. Until they met at Millie's funeral.

Millie sent George to live with her sister Flo in Manningtree, then worked at Osram's lightbulb factory throughout the war. When an incendiary bomb hurtled through her bedroom ceiling, she put out the fire without fuss, and went back to bed. Her home never changed, a delight for great nieces on London holidays. Great Auntie Millie showed Cousin Pauline and me the London sights. Pigeon feeding in Trafalgar Square, duck feeding in St James's Park, elephant feeding at the zoo, and eating cheese sandwiches in graveyards. Auntie Millie had a fascination with death. We cringed, on her chosen visit to Madam Tussauds, at stories of Jack the Ripper and Crippen's Murders in the Bath. Her favourite walk home from Baron's Court tube station was through the local graveyard, where we learnt the scandalous stories of her old neighbours: gossips, thieves, bomb victims, pub owners and drinkers. At night, as I woke petrified, haunted by axe murderers, and shaken by underground rumbles, Auntie Millie appeared torch in hand, in floral nightdress, hairnet and rollers, face shiny with cold cream, to cuddle me back to sleep.

Millie's flat held her life. Bookcases of ancient Penguin detective and mystery novels, with every possible Agatha Christie.

Frank and Joan Watson
and Auntie Millie Kemp
(nee Reason)

Auntie Millie and cousin
Pauline. Photos taken with my
Box Brownie camera in 1958

Her kitchen and bathroom were combined in a cupboard size room, on the landing. Contents: a small cupboard for preparing gourmet food, a bath with a wooden lid supporting a washing up bowl and a clothes horse with dripping thick lisle stockings and winciette fading pink 'harvest knickers' (gather all within). Her front room had bay windows, a large Edwardian plastered light rose, slightly cracked in the bombings, marble mantelpiece, groaning with family photos, a divan, with apricot candlewick cover, a brass trolley for moving food and dishes, and polished table. In the corner, behind a pull-back curtain, hid an old but gleaming gas cooker. Roast dinners, sponge cakes, sausage rolls, meringues and feasts were conjured up, and enjoyed with a sherry and half pint of stout.

Until her 80's, Millie was a regular visitor to her young sister, Elsie, in Mistley and talked non-stop. When Elsie responded, Millie expressed her opinions forcefully at the same time, never listening to any reply. Her place as beautiful younger child had been stolen by this cuckoo in her nest. Somehow Millie felt transformed into the ugly sister. But they were the two survivors of a powerful sisterhood. Neither would tolerate a word against the other. Both were warm and loving.

My lasting image is of both jostling to cuddle my baby daughter, Jenny, their great-great niece, holding up their arms the highest to bounce Bessie's great granddaughter on their knees. Elsie was more sprightly and won. Millie drew her lips tightly together and boasted about George, about to become an admiral!

53: Fish and visitors

My mother Joan dished up meals with love.
Our dining room table was a safe place:
good plain 50s food, no frills,
predictable, good-humoured meals.
Rationing ruled and good manners reigned.
"You'll get worms if you eat raw vegetables."
"Knife and fork together when you finish. "
"Milk in a jug, no bottles on the table ,"

After a fragile gestation
I was squeezed out, shocked and skeletal,
in a touch and go forceps birth
Joan determined to feed me up:
bountiful breast milk, then Farley's rusks,
meals followed by a spoon of sticky Virol,
cod liver oil and orange juice concentrate.
Tinned spaghetti, baked beans,
sardines, tomatoes, all on toast
rang the daily teatime changes,
completed by home made sponge,
marzipan Battenberg, or Penguin biscuits.
I ate it all, apart from white of egg,
but school dinners filled no holes:
soggy cabbage, beef gristle,
tapioca with red jam, frogs spawn,
lumpy mash, limp lettuce and boiled egg.
Solid egg white hidden under my knife,
the Dinner ladies met silent resistance.
Miss Pritchard, the headmistress, cajoled
"No playtime until you submit"
She force fed me white of egg, I gagged,
sprayed Miss Prichard's shoes
green and yellow with white of egg.
My ribs remained skeletal cages.

"Jack Sprat could eat no fat,
his wife would eat no lean. "
As Joan fed me up, she dieted.
then gravitated back to comfort food.
Squeezed in well fitting corsets,
despairing, tried different regimes;
counted calories, ate grapefruit,
then blue pills from the doctor.
Became tetchy on double speed.
ran for the Sunday bus in high heels,
beat the clock in half normal time.
Exhausted with palpitations,
returned to egg and energy roll diet.
I stayed skinny, Joan remained plump:
both relished Cadburys milk chocolate.
a ration bonus from Mr. King the grocer.
warmed by Joan's bounteous smile.

Joan repeated well loved meals:
chops and potatoes for Sunday roast,
mint sauce with lamb, apple with pork,
homegrown broad or runner beans.
Joyful arrival of a fridge in 1958.
brought Birds Eye frozen peas;
no more shelling, or picking
maggots from over ripe pods.
Frozen ice lollies and jelly that set;
chickens no longer just for Christmas.

Joan eagerly taught me to cook.
eager to bake sponge cake.
Mouth dripping in anticipation.
no scales needed: an ounce was
a heaped tablespoon of flour or
a level desert spoonful of sugar,
Butter and sugar double beaten,

189

flour sifted to aerate the sponge.
Delicious, but Joan warned me
"Cake makers can't bake pastry".
Her perfect home-made sausage rolls
baked with readymade puff pastry
wrapped around skinless sausages!

Friction arose when I attempted 60s recipes.
American and European ideas had crept in.
I tried Maryland chicken and corn cakes.
All went well, I was confident.
"You can't cook chicken without roasties"
"We don't need them, there's plenty "
"Don't be stupid. I'll peel potatoes"
My self-control evaporated. I shouted.
Threw my Mother's best wedding hat.
It missed her, but landed in the cats milk.
No more cookery experiments for me.

"Fish and visitors stink after three days;"
 was auntie Millie's favourite saying.
Joan and Frank welcomed guests warmly,
ensured the happiness of family and friends.

Joan felt the strain of being a perfect hostess.
Once, on the third day, timing gone astray.
over fraught breakfast, I explained the delay,
"Mum is just scraping the soot off the toast "
Laughter ceased when Joan's face
showed she did not share the joke.

Joan cooked tried and tested recipes,
from her trusted well-turned 1957
Good Housekeeping Cookery Compendium.
New dishes were borrowed from friends:
specialities, Frangipani, a secret recipe,
Chicken Marengo and Baked Alaska.

Joan only left a few hand copied recipes,
including the family Christmas pudding.
adopted from Auntie Elsie as she aged,
tucked in her pristine Good Housekeeping.
Her only other hardly looked-at cookbook.
'Delia Smith Christmas Recipes', a gift from me.
All her best recipes stored in her head.

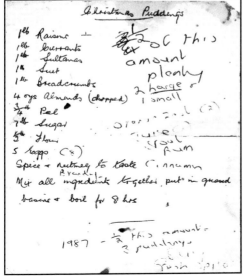

Whilst...

I own two groaning shelves of cookbooks:
opening at encrusted favourite recipes,
from Jamie, Leon, Mildred's, World Café.
and Not Just a Load of Old Lentils.
Watercress soup from Cranks,
Courgette and Lentil Gratin and
Nutty Onion Flan (from Sarah Brown 1988).
Plus my Good Housekeeping Cookbook,
a first wedding gift from Joan in 1969,
spattered with bread sauce and marble cake,
with an aroma of cloves and chocolate.
No longer skinny, I am rounded like Joan.

54: Novices abroad in 1962

Invisible holiday snapshots trawled,
from deep in my memory store.
My mother joyfully weeps, overawed
in a purple shadow mountain valley:
streams cascade from snow-iced caps,
paths coil to Heidi's story-book chalet,
goat-bells beckon me to clamber.
But onwards our Cosmos Coach
battles to the next comfort stop,
On to conquer 7 countries in 14 days!

Belgium, drab and dirty.
Liechtenstein, a sneeze,
Luxembourg, a long toilet queue.
Germany, autobahns and order,
Liebfraumilch and pumpernickel.
but, my father relives the war.
Bier Keller lager: a small German
leers, makes obscene gestures
at my plump blonde mother,
My tall kind dad rises to full height,
"Englander, blitz, ack, ack, bang."
My shock. Cringe. Quick retreat.
On to conquer 7 countries in 14 days.

Austria, cream cakes and cowbells.
Smiles freeze on the Gotthard Pass,
harem-scarum on hairpin bends,
reverse over the ravine edge,
glacier glimpse, white knuckle
Helter-skelter spectacular ride.
My mother's hackles rise,
as the border guard surveys
our family passport, and grins

"Bella Sheila Elizabeta bambino no."
At 14. noticed at last, not a child any more.
On to conquer 7 countries in 14 days!

Italy, ancient olive groves, vines,
women, in black, scrub clothes
in rock-strewn streams. Poverty.
Begging priests, stray dogs siesta,
heat-mist. Minestrone soup,
spaghetti not tinned, taste heaven.
Tourists torture, rustic toilets
mere holes in the ground,

My mother storms out of the Doges Palace,
across the Bridge of Sighs, angered
by rich cruel rulers painted next to God.
Gondola sonata. My bottom pinched,
forced to walk in between my parents.
"You are treating me like a child!"
On to conquer 7 countries in 14 days!

A faded French hotel in Nice,
Beach gigolos and glamour girls,
plotting to get Amsterdam diamonds
from their sugar daddies
My first gentle kiss with the page boy,
Tearful farewell waves. Chateaux,
Dijon mustard, Eiffel Tower.
Cross channel ferry, White Cliffs
My mother smuggles an extra
half of orange liqueur, a criminal:
addicted to continental trips.
Case permanently half packed
Imodium, travel kettle, phrase books,
hair rollers and net, sun cream,
toilet paper, corset and stockings.

Joan with her friend Jill Piper at the
Villa Carlotta, Lake Como.

I caught the travel bug,
On to visit 40 countries in 70 years.
and still counting!

Sheila Kelly 08.12.2018
The centenary of my mother, Joan Watson's birth.

55: Like mother like daughter?

Joan dressed me in love and home-made clothes. Clothes sewn with precision and style in post war austerity. Smocked, Peter Pan collared, or puff-sleeved. Joan was not going to have anyone look down on us. She knitted new swimming costumes for me and my friend, Hilary. Entranced and involved as Joan unwound old jumpers on to upturned chair-legs, I relaxed. Old knitting imprinted in the skeins as up and down waves. I stretched out my hands to carefully hold a skein, as Joan rolled perfect wool balls. "What a good girl to help mummy." I basked in the praise and warm smile, But Joan often found fault with me "why, when you can be angelic, can you also be so naughty and strong-willed. Sheila why have you snipped half your golden waves off? Frank you were meant to be looking after her, not fast asleep?'

Beach photos carefully posed by Hilary's dad, show me, digging in the sand, in

a striped costume, knitted proudly by Joan. Calamity. Splashing through the waves, my wet costume stretched, before sinking to the sand. I looked at mum's tight face; knew it must be my fault. Relief, everyone laughed, even Joan shaking with warm unstressed giggles. Always unpredictable.

Clothes were a constant source of tension. An expensive red corduroy pinafore dress, handed down by Joan's posh friends. 'Only to be worn for best.' I begged to wear it. Ink splashed on the front. Fear loomed. Disaster could be averted by picking off the velvet pile. Yet another telling-off. "You don't deserve lovely clothes." I was shamed and sorry. Joan was determined I would not go off the rails. Stepping out of the front door was always a nightmare, "Lift your shoulders up or you'll be round shouldered."

At 8, Cousin Pauline and I were chosen as bridesmaids for cousin Val. Life became a delight of meetings about rosebud bridesmaid dresses that Joan offered to make. The dining table full of precisely pinned patterns, speedy clattering of the Singer machine handle, and rewinding the bobbin in even faster frenzy. Perfect results. Happiness engulfed the prospective wedding. Pride goes before a fall. On the morning of the wedding, I put on new scalloped-edge white socks, ran down the garden and trod on a nail, piercing my foot. 'I won't be a bridesmaid if I tell.' I stemmed the flow of blood with a hankie. Changing time came, smiles became frowns, Joan shouted "What have you done now, Sheila? You will get tetanus, you won't be a bridesmaid." Frantic tears calmed by dad, who had plasters. Joan had spare socks of course. The wedding photos show a smiling family, never a cross word!.

L to R: Kitty Taylor, Sheila Watson, Val Seager, Pauline Cook, Eileen Jenkins (nee Seager)

197

I tried to live up to expectations. After years of knitting lessons, tears caught in unravelling stitches, I wanted to knit on my own. I was 13 after all. A long green jacket loosely knit. "Make sure the tension is correct."A floor-length jacket, never worn. "You never ever listen, do you Sheila?"

Later: compromise, We chose fabrics and patterns together from Liberty's sale. Success. Incredible mini-dresses for teacher-training college, made entirely by Joan. Edwardian style, high necked, leg of mutton sleeves, navy and mustard striped seersucker and small fabric covered buttons. Harmony. Pink and green polka dot mini dress. Purple, green, blue, and mustard lightly striped woollen dress worn with coloured tights. My dad called me 'Merry-legs.' A shot silk, empire-line first wedding dress. Although I had to be chivvied to buy some suitable shoes two days before the wedding. " Why are you so disorganised?"

A 25 year old clothes rebel butterflied out of a short-lived marriage. I made long tiered Laura Ashley flowered dresses, wore striped socks and clogs. A student-again, on release from teaching, with a year's full pay to study for an Education degree in 1974. Elsie, my godmother taught me to crochet. Joan did not crochet so I could play with the yarn in complex patterns, without comparing myself to Joan's perfection. Adorned in shawls, crocheted whilst discussing Piaget, social inequality and Jungian philosophy. I was well camouflaged at Goldsmiths College in the mid 1970s, where the height of comic sartorial elegance was the long haired student wearing odd coloured socks for his final exams. Freedom. At a family wedding, I wore a borrowed, tie-dyed, long velvet cloak. Friction. Visiting posh family friends led to a written letter of warning, "you looked like a clown."

Jenny's birth created a truce. Joan knitted baby cardigans, sewed up Cloth Kit pinafore dresses and dungarees, bought enthusiastically, by her 'disorganized' daughter, with no time to sew up the kits. I had woven baby shawls for friends' babies, sadly using scratchy wool. But never finished the crochet granny shawl for my own baby. Uncertain how to join the squares together, that shawl is still hidden in a pile of unfinished goods at the bottom of the wardrobe.

We visited a coalminers's cottage at Beamish Museum, in 1993. Second heaven for me, a rag-rug by the hearth just like the ones Auntie Flo made from old clothes, including undies; a rag-rug for every baby in the family. Even a garden with vegetables in straight lines, just like my dad grew. Jenny ran down the garden and squealed, she had stepped in new white trainers into a pile of soot. Joan had died two months before, but her words sprang out of my mouth and echoed between generations. "What have you done now? You never look where you're going."

Jenny the ClothKit Kid

Sheila in hippy kit in 1975

56: My first wedding

It was the night before my wedding. All was ready in our house: In my bedroom hung my empire-line wedding dress, skilfully hand-made by my mother, in stylish shot-silk, a bargain from Liberty's. Underneath stood white silk shoes, only bought two days before: an inevitable portent (no escape for runaway brides wearing high heeled Cinderella shoes). Downstairs, best friends relaxed, enjoying Liebfraumilch and salad with tinned salmon. A knock at the door revealed the in-laws, uninvited guests, bearing champagne. Laughter faded as the colonel's stature blocked the door, and his wife hovered. My father fetched a corkscrew, and the blustering ex-colonel looked down his nose askance that my dad lacked the knowledge to open champagne. I felt intimidated by the arrival of the aliens, judged and sentenced by my future in-laws. At our first meeting, when I was just 17, the large moustached colonel, had overfilled my glass, then boomed at me as Harvey's Bristol Cream dripped on his priceless Persian carpet, "You clumsy girl, this rug cost £2000." '*Whilst our new home only cost £1900.*' An impenetrable ex-colonial class barrier existed, but tender-hearted, I had felt sorry for the long haired unloved boy imprisoned in boarding school, whilst his parents lived just down the road. Forbidden to go to art school, too rich for a grant, he was now stagnating and snarling as a solicitor's clerk. An optimistic bride, I imagined I could make my disenchanted groom happy.

After the invasion we relaxed in familiar harmony, which I was to leave for ever. I shivered in anticipation. This wedding did not feel blessed. None of my bridal fairy godmothers could be there to provide protection, Auntie Elsie and Great-auntie Flo were ill, and Mrs. Abrahams, my wise socialist college lecturer, was busy elsewhere, although she sent a telegram. Still I imagined riding into the sunset with my knight on a white charger. Foolish dreamer.

As we approached the church, my father tried rescuing me "It's not too late to change your mind". Apprehension ignored, I smiled in anticipation as we trudged through sludge, under chauffeur held umbrellas against the drizzle. Red velveted bridesmaid cousins were comforting, and my father escorted me up the aisle to a joyful "Oh Come all You Faithful."The groom did not smile. He took my arm in ownership, a new possession.

L to R: bridesmaid Kaye Taylor, the best man, the in-laws, the groom, the bride, Frank, Joan and bridesmaid Mandy Taylor

Reader, I married him. What a mistake. The photos, in a silver and gold embossed album, now buried in the back of our wardrobe, show a young bride in hairpiece embedded with white flowers, smiling over-happily with head on one side, detached from her inner doubts, and a dissatisfied groom. Few smiles on his face. Whilst the guests enjoyed the buffet, we shivered outside, with close family, for an hour for photos only viewed in the first flurry of excitement, and later to become a painful reminder after the divorce. Then forgotten in decades of new love, children, time and clutter.

We even missed the moment when Great–auntie Millie misjudged her chair and four men tried to pull her up, whilst her long 'harvest' drawers were visible to all. Our side of course, the groom's family looked aghast: I was lost in the chasm in the middle. As I changed into my going away fur-coat, a student bargain from Deptford Market; Diddie, an elderly family friend and fortune teller, crept in, with unwanted wise advice "You think your life is going very smoothly at the moment, but you are going to have to gather up all your resources and start all over again."

No fairy godmothers blessed this wedding, or spun a spell to restore shattered dreams and illusions. Three years later, I did have to 'start again:' my bridegroom was tempted by the excitement of new love at Clacton Teacher Training College, an unlikely venue. Like Bessie, I found myself rejected at 24, by my trusted love, and forced to travel a different path. Bessie's legend haunted me, I floundered, worried early death awaited me as well. I discovered divorced women were still social outcasts in 1972. I questioned my worth, lost confidence

BUT...

Supportive, loving new and old friends rescued me from self pity. Whilst I continued to love teaching, I travelled down alternative routes, became a weekend hippy.; I enjoyed weaving, leylines, folk music and festivals, astrology, and vegetarian food.

Then I returned to University and studying. I asked questions about politics, inequality, feminism, war, and racism. My mother was aghast at her wayward daughter, and even asked "are you immoral, Sheila?" I assured her I was perfectly normal. She looked doubtful. I cautiously explored new relationships (not always the right choices, as I undervalued myself, and was wary of being hurt again). I travelled to prove I could cope by myself: a mini-van overland trip to Greece and Turkey, when I caught fleas, from a fellow traveller's Afghan sheepskin jacket, and the shits from insanitary toilets: life's lessons.

Although the marriage break up was painful at the time, I can now look back and realise it opened up my life for the better, If that first wedding had lasted we would have both been suffocated. My smiles would have become external not internal. I would have missed real love, the joy of my daughter being just who she is, and life's bonus, loving my step-children and grandchildren.

50 years later, buried inside the old wedding album, I found a card signed by the grooms' work colleagues, all strangers, apart from one name that danced in surprise, my second mother-in-law. As one door closes, a window opens.

57: Rhubarb Jam

Bessie's Recipe 157
To every pound of rhubarb allow 1lb of sugar,
the rind of half a lemon, and to every 12lbs
allow 1 lb. of almonds.
Wipe the rhubarb dry and cut it up, put it
into the preserving pan, with the grated lemon
rind, & the almonds, blanched and chopped.
Boil 1 to 1 1/2 hours. Must be well skimmed.

24 July 1979, 2 Spurgeon Street
A large bundle of thick stalked, large leaved, rhubarb abracadabred on the
back doorstep last night. Recompense probably from a guilty thief? On
Saturday, half our verdant crop of spinach was harvested and vanished, cut
straight by a knife, not nibbled by rampant rabbits enjoying a midnight feast.
What to do with this unwanted exchange? Cooking rhubarb jam would provide
a remedy for surplus fruit, and busy forgetfulness on a quiet summer holiday
day. I needed to distract myself from my miscarriage three months before

Ruby red rhubarb promising new delights.

On the table lay a copy of my grandmother Bessie's recipe book, which she
enthusiastically collected and wrote out, when a young kitchen-maid. Inherited
by Millie, her next younger sister, now my elderly great aunt. 60 years later,
Millie busily packed up her Baron's Court home, to live out her last years with
her son in Devon. Still insightful, Millie had observed "I'll always grieve for
Ella and Bessie, we were lost sisters without them. Now I live through a net
curtain, life's veiled. I no longer know if people are alive or dead, still it doesn't
matter, as I never see them anyway." Millie, whilst house clearing, had given
my mother Bessie's recipe book. Joan, a law abiding, no-risk school secretary,
illicitly photocopied the recipes at work, for me. The half read folder of carefully
indexed kitchen staples, provided a remedy for my emptiness, with the added
promise of chopped almonds in the jam recipe. Bessie might have needed
a pound of almonds with gluts of rhubarb, picked from the large vegetable
garden at Bradfield Vicarage, when she was a 15 year old kitchen maid. Only

4 oz. needed today, quarter recipe quantities. (When Bessie had shown her new recipes to her frugal mother, Emily amazed, ventured "Whoever wastes almonds in jam. Well, I never.") My Sainsbury's value packet of almonds were even already skinned and blanched. Life eased by mountains of supermarket food.

A treat in store. I never use scales for cooking, all measures are by spoon or comparison. Whilst by law I taught metric weights at school to my infants, bags of sugar were still sold in pound weight. The rhubarb was roughly 3lb, after washing and chopping, leaves thrown in the dustbin, as they would poison the compost. Cheese graters are perfect for grating lemon rind. Bessie's recipe didn't state whether to include the juice, but I decided the Edwardian maxim would be 'waste not, want not' so I squeezed it in. I believe it adds pectin, the magic setting ingredient. A slow simmer, whilst adding sugar gradually, and well stirred to avoid burning. Bash the packet of whole almonds with a rolling pin, the lazy way to chop nuts

Grey-green sludge needed constant skimming from the pan.

A uniformed figure clouded the open back door. A large midwife looked at me suspiciously "Are you Sheila Robins? I'm here for your 6 month check-up." She glanced at my dungarees and flat stomach. My face blanched to match the almonds. "You don't look very far gone." Angry, sad and good mannered, I apologised. "I had a miscarriage in April, you should have been informed. I was in hospital, and the consultant knew." No words of sympathy. "I should have been told. What a wasted journey." The black shadow departed the back door, leaving a chasm of loss.

Thick suds bubbling down the saucepan. Rushing upstairs, throwing myself on the bed, tears and anger merged into swearing.

Three months ago, I lay in this bed for 10 days trying to keep my baby safe in spite of blood trickling. Dr. Withnall, my new young GP had arrived out of breath, to check on me concerned, but with a wry sense of humour: "I don't keep fit. If God had wanted us to jog, we'd have been born in trainers." The next day a bucket was borrowed from the neighbour, when I started to pour blood. A rush to hospital, where I was asked if I needed some 'bunnies': hospital talk for sanitary towels. A supportive group of women filled the ward. Maud facing her fifth miscarriage, and older women needing hysterectomies. All showed kindness to a 16 year old in for an abortion. Support. No judgement here amongst this magnificent cohort of women. A student nurse held my hand through the labour pains of miscarriage. Wheeled across the open courtyard at midnight to the theatre for a scrape. Discharged the next morning. Someone else already in my hospital bed before my lift arrived. I sat on a plastic chair just waiting and gazing.

The smell of burnt sugar. Ruined rhubarb jam. Not much left between skimming froth and a burnt saucepan bottom. Only two small jars of toffee flavoured jam with over toasted almonds.

Not the outcome I wanted.

58: Lost in our back garden in 1986

An old man shambles down the back door step, grips onto the door post, and needs my arm for support. I wonder 'Where has my dad gone?' Once smart, upright, tall, my hero. Now strands of hair fall over his eyes, while toothpaste spittle and marmalade adorn his jumper. Stale smell hidden by aftershave. No Sunday tie, no polished shoes. Dad wears slippers, easier to pull on and off. He can no longer dress himself, and needs my mum to help and cajole him out of pyjamas into daytime clothes.

We shuffle on our oft repeated path, where dad shows off his gardening successes in his carefully planned garden, established and loved over 35 years. I play my role, a delusion of normality
"Your runner beans have made a good start, dad, Four leaves already. I've only just planted mine." A small grin, but his eyes are dull, unsmiling, disconnected, "Got to time them well to avoid the frosts." He repeats old sayings. As normal, the bean strings are carefully hung opposite the back door, easy for my mum to pick fresh for lunch. But Jim, the weekly gardener, has planted beans and hung the strings this year, not my dad.

A remembered shriek from the shed, where once a mouse was disturbed from his bed as dad pulled on his wellie boots. Every day, dad put on his cycle clips and dragged his bicycle out of the shed, and rang his bell as he set off to work, while Ginger leapt alongside on the stone gate posts.

Past the outside toilet where dad brewed his own beer, until the day he proudly brought in his new brew to taste. The bottle exploded lather all over the newly decorated front room, Ginger licked his fur and circled at increasing speed drunkenly round the house.
Past the drain, where I helped dad empty the remaining bottles, under my mother's eagle eye. His last batch of home-brew.

Across the well cut grass, with an old roller rusting in the corner, once used by dad after he turned the soil, rooted out bindweed, horse tails, dandelions, webs of crouch grass, before planting seed, and nurturing his lawn. Distracted by the past, I spy a small girl, missing front tooth, swirling to silent music, curtsying to imagined audiences, a would-be ballet star in pumps and striped socks. Dad stoops slowly to pull up a dandelion and I steady his straightening.

Snow blossom swirls down from next door's greengage tree. Under the mottled white blossom carpet, from a deep memory hole, burrowed to find Roman remains, triumphs a young me, waving my archaeological find, a smokey green, ginger pop bottle, with a marble stopper.

We climb dad's precisely home-built, stepped concrete path, with crisscross pattern to prevent slipping, to the compost heap at the bottom of the garden. Young cowboys, imaginary friends from the past, chase Robin Hood fleetingly, in and out of the blackcurrant bushes. Fresh mint and rhubarb mingle with lemon perfumed elder blossom and the acid scent of fresh grass.

Dad proudly glances at the new potato plants "I reckon my potatoes will be on the dinner table before Uncle Frank's this year. Good Friday is always the best day for planting".
"You must be proud, they're so healthy looking." I try not to shatter his pride and hope of winning the long established competition, but I remember Uncle Frank died 5 years ago, and dad read at his funeral

Dad pauses suddenly and gazes around "I know this is a funny question, but whose garden and house is this?"
"Well, yours and mum's."
"What, do I live here with my mum?"

I am lost for words. My dad is confused by Alzheimer's.

Soon after dad was admitted to a geriatric ward at Severalls Hospital; after he woke one night, screaming at my mother "Who are you, don't kill me" and locked himself in the bedroom. He shambled through his last year, often thinking he was back at work as a mental health nurse, "it's about time I had a day off, I'm always on duty." Mum visited him every day, braving the never-ending dark corridors to reach the welcoming, kind, light courtyard ward. Dad remained aware at times of other's feelings. I kept secret that my relationship with Jenny's dad was disintegrating, but dad asked "Who's been upsetting you then?" In another moment of lucidity, Frank turned to Joan, "I have loved you ever since the moment I first saw you. You are my wife and my life." We smiled and wept silently, along with nearby staff.

In a long night vigil, Frank drifted in and out of death, reluctant to leave us. A healing male nurse held his hand mid-morning, and gave him the peace to depart. My mother walked to the ward's end and screamed one wild wail. The only time she expressed her grief. As usual she inwardly buried her loss. "If I start crying, I'll never stop." Mum then competently gathered up her handbag, to meticulously organise dad's funeral.

For me, I had mourned the loss of my father during the last two dissolving years of his life. After he died, I was able to remember him in the round. Photos returned his whole life.

Frank with big brother Cecil Watson about 1914

Frank and Joan Watson 1970

59: Shuffle the cards

Shuffle the cards to find the past.
Dad's well-used Canasta cards,
found buried in the middle drawer.
adorned with stern royals, and jocular joker,
'The Colourful Card Game from Latin America'.

I remember

dad, mum, family friends playing to win,
laughter, chatter, and rivals drinking gin.
Excluded, a child wide awake in bed,
ear-twitching, eager to creep downstairs.
I regret dad never taught me Canasta.
I open the box with caution, to find my dad.

But am amazed to find myself instead:
hiding alongside hearts and spades are
score cards, from dad's early Alzheimer's days,
of games played with me, an adult pupil,
numbers correctly entered and added by my dad.
Our memories erased, my card sharp dad won!

Deal the pack, back to the past.
My dad first played Canasta to relax
as the Eighth Army liberated Italy,
to forget the stench and shots of battle.

I remember
Auntie Millie, fireside chair ensconced,
never lost once at Clock Patience,
making order out of a chaotic world.
My tarot cards too powerful to hold,
predicted miscarriage and dismay,
now hidden away to dispel their power.
My last sad card game with my dad,
unable to shuffle or understand the rules,
playing Donkey with my infant daughter.
Hidden jokers had dealt dementia.

Be careful when you shuffle the pack,
cards have neither top nor bottom,
and double faces that gaze two ways,
both backwards and forwards,
into the past and future at once.

60: Dancing through life

A struggle to be born,
placenta, part lost at six months.
Held upside down,
I was a weak skinned rabbit,
slapped to induce life.
After 20 minutes, a feeble cry,
a heartbeat, the rhythm of my life:
I would dance to this new tune.

"No more children, Mrs. Watson,
Neither you or your baby would survive,"
Dr. Sauvan-Smith advised,
as he sewed up my mother,
over small steel rimmed glasses,
Slightly brain damaged at birth,
poorly co-ordinated, slow walking,
"Butter fingers" at catching,
I would dance when I found the right tune.

Down at the Empire Cinema, a flea pit,
my first film was the 'Red Shoes.'
Enchanted by Moira Shearer,
I wanted to dance in red ballet shoes.

Just three ballet lessons after school.
I learnt every step to perform
'Goldilocks and the Three Bears.'
Always late, rushed after work
my mother lowered the axe
"Not enough time or money.
Red ballet shoes are too costly".
But I wanted to dance in the ballet.

Belle of the Ballet starred in Girl Comic.
On the Corporation double-decker bus,
I called upstairs to my imaginary friends,
Belle and a whole ballet ensemble,
"Our stop next. Time to dance home."
"People think you are a silly little girl,"
warned my embarrassed mother.
I danced down the street in unison
with Belle and her invisible troupe.

60 years later, Valli, our neighbour,
a witness to my lost childhood,
remembered me dancing outside
spinning to never ending silent music.
A gift of striped German socks, worn
with new red sandals empowered me.
At last, I danced in red shoes.

Ballroom dance lessons at school:
I was tall and only learnt the boy's part.
"No Strictly Come Dancing for me."
Hand jiving and the locomotion
gave us solidarity "girl-power".
At 13, in Auntie Flo's kitchen,
my cousins and I learnt the twist,
pulling sideways with gripped towels
We danced to a new modern beat!

Married to men, who heard their own tunes,
we danced out of step

Single again, an invite to clog-dance.
My mother warned "You won't get the job,
If you dance in the street
in red clogs and striped socks.

No Headteacher wears parrot earrings,
or carries a ducks head umbrella"
I proved her wrong!
Ranting through Rochester Sweeps Festival, Scarborough,
Colchester and Norwich,
I belonged to a real dance team.
In Robin Hoods Bay
we did not miss a step
as donkeys heading to the beach
trotted through our midst.
In my second hand clogs I would dance and rant forever.

An extended hold at a barn dance led
to my new marriage dance, to "Lady in Red."

Long ago, my mother met my father,
foxtrotting at the tennis-club dance.
and waltzed through life in step
For her funeral, Joan
 chose "Lord of the Dance."
A year after she died, an echo,
Chelmsford Morris Men played
"Lord of the Dance," a timely reminder.
I danced, cried and remembered.

Clog dancing can damage your knees.
Restricted by my knee replacement,
I taught others the clog dance steps,
One exhausted dancer remarked,
"You remind me of the ballet teacher in Girl".
But that teacher was old, bent with a stick.
Did my pupil not realize
I was still Belle of the Ballet?

 Now I dance to the radio, sitting in a chair,
unable to jump, but arms in rhythm.
I dance through life to an ever changing tune.
Red clogs wait in the wardrobe,
ready for my funeral one day.

61: I love washing lines

Here we go round the washing line.
Drying, wafting, clothes dancing.
upside down, headless acrobats.
Trouser legs kicking, jumper arms waving.
New blue striped nightie first outing,
toothpaste spittle removed, clean.
Satisfaction, order restored,
on a warm autumnal morning.

This is the way we dry our clothes,
hand washed, machine spun.
Jet beaded black lace top, dripping,
with glistening raindrop hem.
Mirrored in autumn dew, pearls
on the drooping smoke-pink fuschia
dance with entangled jade jumper,
in an overcrowded garden.

This is the way we hang out our clothes.
Vibrant, pink yellow, blue plastic pegs,
autumn rotting, left to decay on the line.
Long ago my mum used wooden pegs,
bag stored, pantry door hung,
frugal, valued, picked off the line,
gathered in, ordered, counted.
Back in well remembered times.

This is the way my mum washed clothes
in a weekly washing battle.
Gas copper lit, third attempt.
Clothes boiled, sink rinsed, mangle
squeezed. Sweaty faced, muscles aching.
Next the Sheet-fold dance, ends to

middle, pass corners, out and begin again,
In a steamy sweating kitchen.

Here we go round the world's washing lines.
Memories. Monks' saffron and mulberry robes
meditating on the Dalai Lama's sanctuary lines.
Multi washed, sun soaked family clothes, praying
on makeshift lines, hooked to the back wall
of Lisbon cathedral.

My proud display of sun bleached nappies,
cooked in my new automatic washing machine,
played on my washing line, 40 long years ago
Laundry from time lost, but more to come.
A never ending action song.

Here we go round...

62: Bessie's cookbook lost and found

Bessie's cookbook, lost by me,
her disordered granddaughter.
"I know it's in a safe place,
But where? It can't be found."
Back bedroom drawers opened wide,
not hidden under untuned violins.
not amidst folded old sofa spare cloth.
At last, discovered buried deep
in 50 years of unsorted photos,
squashed memories, jostling to escape.
What relief: "Found it!"

Bessie's sad cookbook, now desiccated,
marbled emerald and ruby cover faded,
colours erased, cardboard displayed.
A once proud leather spine,
leaf print embossed, now frayed,
curled back, unglued, useless.
On last legs, loose pages escape,
trails of binding thread unravel.
End pages dishevelled, disordered.
Bessie's pre-loved cookbook;
front half still bound, ordered.
confused second half in disarray:
Life's mirror.

*The first six recipes in the index are lost in time: the pages
disappeared in interwar years*

*1- Apple Jelly   2-Fish Tartare
3- Scarborough Pudding   4-Orange Pudding
5- Scalloped Kidneys   6- York Pudding*

Bessie wrote with careful handwriting, and indexed all the pages to Recipe 175, but later recipes were mis-numbered in another hand. When Millie inherited her sister's recipe book, she made her own new definitive mark.

Bessie wrote her last recipe Recipe 276 Haddock in Croute, with looped ascenders, and straight descenders. Whilst on the same page, Millie wrote up Recipes 277 and 278; 'Fillets of Sole in Aspic' and 'Strasbourg Cutlets.' Millie wrote in dark letters in heavily pressed pen, with straight upward strokes, descenders looped, the legacy of a new owner.

Haddock Croutes   276
Ingredients. a cooked dried haddock, croutes of fried
bread. some small mushroom & some white sauce
Flip haddock & sieve it mix with enough white sauce
to bind it well together. cook mushrooms in oven with
butter. Heat haddock & sauce spread some on each
croute & put a mushroom on top

          Fillets of sole in aspic   277

Spread fillets of sole with some fresh forcemeat (prink)
cook when cold cut in slices   Line a Timbale
mould with aspic jelly. Then with the slices of
sole. Let set & fill up with aspic jelly. & the
rest of the slices. Turn out & decorate with
chopped aspic jelly.

          Strasburg Cutlets   278.
                                                centre
Have some thick cutlets. make a slit in the centre
of each & fill with a teaspoonful of foie gras mixed with a
little cream. Wrap in paper & braise for half an hour.
Dish up on spinach & decorate with cooked quarters of tomato.
Cover cutlets with glaze & pour some good brown sauce round..

219

Bessie and Millie's cookbook
encloses clues to past lives;
detailed, good spelling, careful notes.
Ordered, Bessie's mistakes are rare,
Only one ink blot on Recipe 232,
smudging Salad a la Cavendish,
From Recipe 169, Chocolate Soufflé
faint smell of chocolate blobs wafts.
splashed and stuck for 100 years.

Inserted inside, in vanishing writing
scrawled on a torn-out notebook,
Bessie's complicated weekly menu,
a heavy workload for a lone cook.
Rich recipes for a village vicarage!

Monday lunch
Roast sirloin of Beef. Roast Ducks
Rabbit Pie, Cassel Pudding Apple Pudding
Stewed fruit. Custard Mould
Monday Dinner
Clear Soup-Fish. Roast Leg of Lamb
Roast Grouse, Jelly Sponge Mould.
Tuesday Lunch
Hot Pot   Chicken Pie   Jam Puffs
Cheese Lettuce Tomatoes Oatcake Toast
Tuesday Dinner
Clear Soup. Fish Fillets of Veal Roast Grouse
Charlotte Russe Meringues Cheese Straws. Omelette
Wednesday Lunch
Roast Neck of Lamb. Roast Ducks Cold Meat
Ruby Pudding. Apple Charlotte Stewed Fruit Junket
Wednesday Night
Soup Fish Roast Leg of Mutton, Toasted Cheese
Friday Night
Mutton Broth. Roast Veal, Cassel Pudding

Saturday Lunch
Irish Stew Cold Veal. Batter Pudding
Stewed Fruit. Milk Pudding
Saturday Dinner
Halibut. Jugged Hare Caramel Pudding. Toasted Cheese
Sunday Lunch
Roast Forequarter of Lamb. Ruby Pudding
Stewed Fruit Baked Custard
Sunday Supper
Cold Lamb Cold Boiled Chicken Pigeon Pie Anchovy Eggs
Rice Cream Stewed Fruit

A wealth of letters hide in the leaves,
shared recipes from faraway cooks,
Breakfast Risotto, Crumpets, Mutton Cutlets,
Sliced Beef with Onions, a religious offering
from the Cathedral Close, Salisbury,
of another over worked, vicarage cook.
Pate from the Manor House, Halesworth,
cut out recipes from servant's magazines.
As the Great War started, still
'The Table' magazine focused   (August 15th 1914)
on cooking in the grouse season!
An unequal world of indulged gentry.

Both sisters were enmeshed by graphology,
"Character Reading from Handwriting."
Magazine cuttings judged unsuspecting victims:

"A man's handwriting, with unmistakable indications of an impetuous nature,
and hot temper, lack of balance and steadfastness of mind,"
"A child of a sweet tempered disposition, whose docility is due not only to her
amiability, but also to an intelligent and reasonable nature."

Sisters eager to discover their future characters
from distinct styles, Bessie careful, Millie forthright.

What Does Your Hand-writing Mean?

If your reply has not already appeared, keep a steady look-out for it in these columns every week, and please remember we are doing our VERY best to get the replies through as quick as possible. IN THE MEANTIME, WE CANNOT OFFER TO GIVE ANY MORE CHARACTER READINGS, SO WILL READERS KINDLY REFRAIN FROM SENDING IN UNTIL WE GIVE THE WORD?

"DAISY OF LEEDS."—Patient, persevering, careful, prudent and cautious, tidy, methodical. You pay great attention to small details. You are loving and affectionate, very reliable, and trustworthy. Generous and kind

"ONE INTERESTED."—Original and clever, economical, careful, prudent, rather good-natured, tidy, practical, have good business ability, like to manage things, and would make a good manageress of any shop. You like comfort and ease, peace and quiet.

HENRY JONES.—Your writing shows ardour and enthusiasm, energy, quickness, wit, sense, and good business ability. You are clever and ingenious, have confidence, self-control, and courage.

WINIFRED.—You are orderly, tidy, methodical, and careful, prudent and cautious, fair and just in all your dealings, but you will ... You do not mind what you pay, but you desire a fair return and full value. You are energetic, quick, persevering, determined, and brave.

MARY.—You have a strong will, and can sometimes be quite obstinate. You like some company and gaiety. You are rather lazy, and do not like to be quick over anything.

"UNDER THE SHADE."—You have a quiet and modest nature, a very strong will, and will be quite determined when you like. You are honest and sincere.

HILDA BURTON.—You are ambitious, and should do fairly well in the world. You have a strong will and a determined character. You like your own way, and usually manage to obtain it. You are fond of comfort and ease, and have much artistic taste.

"BLUEBELL."—You are fair and just towards others, loving and affectionate, honest, sincere, and true.

JEANETTE.—You are very good-natured, affectionate, and loving, a little selfish, and a good judge of character.

WINIFRED THORNTON.—You are economical and careful, patient, and can be very persevering. You like everything tidily done, with method, and in order. You can keep a secret.

BETTY.—You are clever and ingenious, very original, and though you are critical, and sometimes find fault with others, you are good and kind, and have broad ideas.

"KIT."—You are rather lazy, and hate being bothered about things. You can do things well if you are let do them in your own way, and when you feel like it. But as you are very artistic, you will have moods and fancies.

D. WEST.—You have a very tidy and careful nature, methodical, prudent, cautious, fond of routine and order. You are too slow sometimes, and are too particular over little things that really do not matter.

MOLLIE (Carlisle).—You have a very determined, even obstinate, nature. You are quick and rather impulsive, and you are enthusiastic over things you like.

MISS D. PARKIS (envelope).—Painstaking and persevering, kind, loving, gentle, very affectionate and good, a contented and happy nature.

E. MAUD EDWARDS.—Unselfish and kind, refined, gentle, tender, and true. You have literary ability, artistic taste, and good musical talent.

MAUD.—Loving and kind, a very good judge of character, and will be a charming friend. You are honest, sincere, loyal, and true. A little untidy sometimes, but patient and persevering as a rule.

MISS PUTT'S FRIEND.—Your friend likes comfort and ease, things

well done, and without too much economy. He is a little slow in some things, has a good sense of justice and fairness towards others, and would never willingly wrong anyone. He is very artistic.

MISS PUTT.—Unselfish and kind, very affectionate and loving. You have confidence, and like to do things your own way and in your own time. You have an honest and loyal character.

VIOLET.—You have sound common sense, a kind nature, and a reliable, affectionate, and charming disposition. You are incapable of a mean or treacherous action.

"C'EST MOI."—This writer is refined, sensitive, and highly strong. She is clever, can turn her hand to many things, and do them well. She has some affection and love, but will bestow regard on few persons.

OLIVETTE.—Patient and persevering, fond of comfort and ease, also luxury. The nature is very artistic. There is much generosity, also great affection, but only for a chosen few.

"A TOI."—Your writing shows a broad-minded and very go-ahead, though at the same time correct and modest, nature. You are energetic, quick, impulsive, sometimes impatient, and have ardour and enthusiasm ; sociable and chatty.

DOREEN (Yorkshire).—Modest and quiet, like comfort, peace, and ease. You have a strong will, am generous, and like everyone to be happy and comfortable.

"SMILES" (Spennymore).—You are very generous, too much so sometimes. You are rather apt to get down-hearted.

PANSY.—You are original and clever, can be

very energetic and quick,, but you like comfort and ease as a rule. Very sincere and honest, loyal and true, reliable and trustworthy.

"A HONEST LIVING."—You have much patience and perseverance. You are economical and careful, prudent and cautious.

"NANNA" (Motherwell).—Clever, generous, and kind, you like to help others, but you are shy about putting yourself forward. Fair and just.

LILIAN FLORENCE PARROTT.—Sociable and chatty. You have a determined nature, are good-tempered and kind, but may be a little hasty sometimes. You can be economical when it is necessary.

"21 OLD CROSS."—Honest and sincere, very loyal and true, generous and kind, have much affection and love, and a good sense of justice and fairness towards others.

SALLIE.—You are rather untidy and careless, and seem to have a struggle in life against destiny of circumstances, ill-health or worry. You are loving and kind ; like comfort and ease.

"JASSENA."—Your character is not entirely developed. A very sweet and gentle nature, honest, sincere, loyal, and true, very reliable, patient, and persevering. Loving and affectionate.

EMILY (Chester).—Economical, careful, prudent, and cautious. You could never be wasteful or extravagant, but you are rather inclined to look on the black side of things, and seem to have rather a struggle in life against many things.

A. HUGH (Cheshire).—Your character is straightforward and sincere, loyal, honest, and true. You can love devotedly, but do not like many. You are rather selfish.

"ESPARANZA."—You have much affection, tenderness, gentleness, loyalty, sincerity, honesty, and generosity. You are determined, and have a strong will.

(Continued on page 26.)

222

Moving after 50 years from her London home,
Millie gave the cookbook to her niece Joan,
Bessie's daughter, organised, confident,
but disturbed by this unwanted gift.
A reminder of her wanton, useless, rejected mother.
Joan resented her mother's death, abandoned,
to playground name calling, "bastard, orphan."
Now Joan found herself reflected in the recipes,
practical, ordered, planned, thoroughly tested.
Joan tossed away her previous perceptions.
Bessie was caring, organised, enjoyed cooking,
Joan was her mother's daughter.
Maybe she was loved!

Joan, photocopied Bessie's cookbook for me;
replaced the missing back cover with a mounted
school photo of her much loved, treasured
eleven year old Granddaughter Jenny,
already an eager cook.
Nana amused her as a toddler,
with her magic trick of cooking
chocolate cornflake cakes,
in the cold fridge!
At eleven, Jenny became a vegetarian:
in a new 'woke' generation.

63: Daughter, mother, grandmother

A family does not speak of a disgraced person... someone we don't talk about.
A ghost seems to leave the tomb and manifest itself (in a descendant)
after one or two generations.
What haunts are not the dead, but the gaps left within us by the secrets of others.
It is because a son or daughter has not assimilated the unfinished mourning of someone.
The phantom is a formation of the unconscious that has never been conscious
from an unspeakable secret belonging to another.
The Ancestor Syndrome : Anne Ancelin Schutzenburger

Part one: my invisible grandmother
Our ancestors are cradled inside us,
embraced, encompassed by the deceased.
Rooted in our matriarchal family,
branching from the Maltster's five daughters,
Flo, Bessie, Millie, Elsie and Ella.
At funerals we recognise long-lost cousins.
They have turned into their mothers,
wear the same faces, gestures, voices.
Joan, my mother, is etched in my face.
Grandmothers resurface once more.
Daughter, mother, grandmother mirrored,
spun in a web of invisible threads
in repeating patterns, rhythms and tales.

Bessie, my invisible grandmother
walked alongside my hesitant steps.
Her photos hidden, never mentioned:
a dire warning, outcome of a sinful life,
buried in dark cupboard depths, with
my hidden pop-up 'Red-Riding Hood.'
Wolf's snarling jaws, snapping teeth
had devoured my grandma. *Was I next?*

All my cousins had grandmothers,
grandfathers were an absent breed.
A curious child, I asked questions,
"Where are my grandparents?"
A hasty reply "They're all dead."
Yet Great Aunties Flo, Elsie and Millie
were willing underground conspirators,
ready to retrieve and remember the dead
"Your nana, Bessie, was our loving sister."
Flo searched for Bessie in me:
"You smile like Bessie your nana.
Your voice even sounds like hers."
I longed for tales of the five sisters' past.
Joan tightened her lips, closed her ears,
only opened her heart in later years:
"Bessie made me an orphan and a bastard.
I hated my mother. She abandoned me."

Joan concerned I would be like Bessie,
forbade me to ride a bike, in case I fell;
warned me often of the dangers of sex;
screamed at me for three hours, when
she rooted out my contraceptive pills.
Twenty and engaged, but "off the rails,
just like Bessie your grandmother."
At 21, I married, Joan was relieved,
believed *I couldn't shame her now*

But my marriage floundered,
a student again, back to college,
enjoyed a late teenage rebellion at 25.
Questioned for hours about any lovers.
"Where do you think my boyfriend sleeps?"
"You've broken your father's heart."
I stood my ground, found my voice:
read 'Germaine Greer, Jung and Marx,'
became a feminist, socialist, a gentle rebel.

Joan and I visited Elsie, Millie and Flo.
I dressed in smart maroon long skirt,
matching cape and button-up boots.
Millie spoke "Good God girl, what a shock.
thought you were Bessie for a moment,
in fancy boots and 'hobble-skirt."
Joan lips pursed, glared in disapproval.
'Would Bessie never disappear?'
Rooted in the family. I belonged, but
feared 'Was I Bessie's reincarnation.'
Breathed in relief to live past 25,
the age of Bessie's tragic death.

Part two: mother and daughter
I became a weaver and protester
teacher and learner,
well entrenched in feminism,
maternalism not paternalism,
embedded in a loving relationship:
'Marriage an outdated convention.'
Joan strangely made no comment,
longed to be a grandmother,
later supported me through miscarriage at 30,
but then rejoiced in granddaughter Jenny's birth.

As I slept in post-Caesarean sedation,
my parents gazed in wonder for an hour,
explained."She's our first grandchild."
"We realised" grinned the nurses.
Jenny provided reconciliation and truce,
an end to rebellion and most criticism,
the burial of Bessie's silent ghost.

Supportive years, dad lost in Alzheimer's,
my mother visited him daily in Severalls,
through two long years of deterioration.
Joan: always smart, set blond hair
handbag over arm, and caring.
A disturbed patient yelled out
 "Mrs. Thatcher, is there a God?"
We laughed at the mistaken identity.
Unfazed, never word-lost, Joan responded
"Look at the beautiful trees, God is everywhere"
We watched over Frank on a last night vigil.
Reluctant to leave us, he departed slowly.
Joan screamed, one heartfelt farewell,

but never showed her grief again.
"If I start crying, I'll never stop,"
After practiced years of burying emotions,
Joan busied herself in funeral preparations.

Three generation holidays followed,
Joan and Jenny, with me in the middle,
looking both ways, past and future,
mother and daughter, caring for both.
Removed glasses from my snoozing mother,
then splashed in the hotel pool with Jen.
I was bitten slightly
(luckily, no rabies lurks in Corfu)
rescuing Jen from a jumping puppy,
nibbling at her Cloth-kit pinafore dress.

Joan, dressed for cafe-culture, not the beach, with Jenny in Crete 1989

Jen helped nana up steep Greek steps.
Joan and Jen played cards for drachma,
we all played at trying out new roles.
All three escaped into love of books,
Kazio Ishiguro, Margaret Attwood, and Enid Blyton.

Joyful laughter, shared gin and tonics,
island boat trips in Rhodes, duty-free,
Byzantine churches, flamenco in Spain.
Jen led us in a bull-ring visit boycott.
Sightsee, shop, scrabble and buffet meals.
honey yogurt, melon, paella and pizza.

Sheila and Joan,Spain 1990, enjoying duty free gin,

Joan courageous with a brain tumour:
a large black shadow on the scan.
Unable to walk, invited friends to the lost ward,
for a coffee morning, chatter and serviettes.
Joan found comfort, "My grandad came last night.
He lifted me up to look in the water-butt.
I felt safe at last." She smiled and dozed.
Hip broken, Auntie Elsie went into hospital.
"Auntie Elsie will never forgive me,
If I die before her."
Joan's last outing was to Elsie's funeral,
dressed up smartly, pushed in wheelchair.
For a short time, the family matriarch.

In life my mother, Joan, gave strong advice,
a constant seagull on my shoulder,
warning, afraid I would go astray,
I battled to express myself, escape her shadow.
Two strong characters determined to win.
Now I repeat her words, reflect her gaze.
At her funeral, proud of providing a proper tea:
triangle sandwiches, no crusts, macaroons,
strawberries, sherry, and cheese straws.
An approving arm hugged my shoulder.
I smiled, turned round, to invisible warmth.
An empty space.

64: Pilgrimage to the Monastery

We reach the Dalai Lama's monastery,
in search of Nirvana, the meaning of life.
Monsoon rain steams in morning sunlight.
Uphill struggle past rainbow market stalls,
tempted by cheap necklaces, silk scarves.
Climb upwards, follow your inner path.
At last a gateway to the monastery,
Thin begging children, poverty,
dust, rubbish, mind the dog shit,
steep concrete steps. Is this it?
Cedar tree platform, azure light.
Breathe, cool mountain breeze.

Circumambulate clockwise, concentrate.
Pilgrims turn prayer wheels, murmur.
I imagine my oldest friend Hilary appears
whilst our dead mothers chatter nearby.
I envy the serenity of meditating Germans,
overseen by golden Buddha statues.
Encircled by birthday gifts for the Dalai Lama,
away, sailing on his Mediterranean yacht.
No past life revelations for me today.
Was I 'Tinker, tailor, soldier, Queen,
elephant, monkey, tangerine?'

I hope for spiritual transformation,
enter a beeswax candle-lit sanctum,
with gleaming polished sandalwood floors,
Two female lamas, aubergine robed,
start to mop. A bucket totters, water pours.
Silence, I hold my breath, anxious.
Our lamas laugh, mop the spillage away.
My life-lesson, 'Find humour, loose guilt,
laugh, and live in the here and now.'

Maroon and saffron gowns flutter
on the monastery washing lines.
Thunder growls, purple clouds glower,
Sanctuary, in the other worldly monastery cafe,
we find mountain herb tea and carrot cake,
watch eagles soar along mountain valleys.
We discover daily and spiritual life in harmony.

65: Times tables

One times five is five.
My first day at school:
boiled cabbage stink,
windows too high to see out.
Abandoned by my mother,
Miss Pritchard, grey, bunned, grim,
grabbed my wrist, 'a kidnapper.'
So I kicked the grim headteacher.
My karma, a life sentence in schools.

Mrs. Plenty's Reception class, Hamilton Road School 1953

Two times five is ten
Escape to the playground:
marble champ, hula hoop queen.
but can't catch, can't run,
last one chosen for the rounder's team.

Three times five is fifteen:
back combed hair, pinned on
beret, kettle steam shrunk.
a pimple on St Paul's.
Mini skirted, first kissed.

Sick on hockey days.
All learning by rote.
Listen, don't ask questions.
Escape in novel reading,
Beatles, Dylan, and LPs,
smoke-filled coffee bars.
Teenage rebels in school uniform.

Four times five is twenty,
Student teacher in the East End:
Board school waiting demolition,
toilets outside through the snow!
Forty infants, three floors up,
sitting in rows, pulling faces,
behind the 70 year old teacher's back.
My task: to take over, teach
groups with topic led curriculum.
Junk box castles, book corner,
science with batteries, bulbs and wire.
to learn with joy and discovery.

Five times five is twenty-five.
Loving teaching in open-plan school:
nature rambles on Greenstead Estate,
Female teachers, forbidden trousers
by our elegant high-heeled headteacher,
rebel in maxi skirts and clogs!
Phone calls warning of IRA bombs,
frequent evacuations onto the field.
Words to learn in tobacco tins!
Conflicting messages.

Six times five is thirty.
Teaching in Wivenhoe, modern maths,
problem solving, story writing. Progress.
Staff call the head by her first name.
Ask questions and learn.

Seven fives are thirty-five:
deputy head at Brightlingsea Infants,
my daughter and class all 4 years old,
muddled roles as mother and teacher.
Eager for equality of opportunity,
I dis-gendered my reception class.
Girls or boys could use both toilets.
Mrs. Brine, cleaner, lover of disaster,
objected "Now them boys
are wetting both toilets"
Equality can have drawbacks.

Eight times five is forty.
Headteacher now to 240 children,
much to my mother's amazement.
"Heads don't have dyed red hair,
or duck head umbrellas,
or clog dance in the street."
"Well, I do."

Nine fives are forty-five.
New library, new computers.
Pulled in many directions in
a thriving community school,
But my mother had a brain tumour.

Ten times five is fifty.
Six months of breast cancer,
Got married, back to school.
Visited schools in Iceland.
New curriculum, more change.

Eleven fives are fifty five.
All management, no time for teaching.
Retirement as a headteacher.
Back to College,
start training as a children's counsellor.

Twelve times five is sixty.
Graduate with a Masters in Education,
parade through Cambridge in my gown.
Joan would have been so proud.
Back to school as a counsellor.

Thirteen fives are sixty five
Counsellor, school governor,
studying art and family history,
Life long learning in the fast lane,
with new knee and walking stick.

Fourteen fives are seventy.
A metal replacement upper spine
pushed me into the slow lane.
I learnt how to walk again.
Back to school once more,
creative writing with the WEA..

Fifteen fives will be seventy five
What next? Watch this space.

Sheila and Julie Lanyon-Hogg, newly M.Eds!

66: Song-lines from the borderlands

"The air is very thin" for fishermen on the Isles of Lewis: life and death dance hand in hand on the shoreline. The last time I saw her my Great Auntie Millie had moved into the Borderlands, "I feel like I'm living with a net curtain wafting in front of me. I picture people but can't remember if they're dead or alive." Always a realist, she chuckled into the day, "Still, it doesn't matter, I never see them anyway".

My oldest friend Hilary has always lived in the Borderlands. 40 years ago she even moved to the edge of the universe, Perth in Australia. A remote waterside city dividing the Indian Ocean from the desert, where Aboriginal song-lines quiver. Aptly they settled in the new suburb named Edgewater. Our story wanders in and out of the borders, in and out of time, to and fro across

the world. Old fables remembered, new tales created in a melody seeking
meaning from the words.

Auntie Elsie, Hilary's mum, my godmother, was born between worlds, able to
see past and future: chatting with dead relatives overnight, reading fortunes
in tea leaved-cups. Other-world white haired and sea-blue eyed holding
ocean depths and spraying surf; Elsie was a water person, from Manningtree
riverside. In contrast, when earth-linked she laughed with her best friend, my
mum Joan, friendship kindled fire-watching in the war. Joan always kept her
feet firmly rooted in the "real" world afraid of the chasms at the edge. Hilary and
I, shawl-wrapped drank our mothers' tunes, kicked off the covers and tumbled,
sister-friends. Every Wednesday, mum and I visited them in Mistley, relishing

crusty home-made bread, and dripping, and new laid double-yolk eggs. A kind day time Georgian house, shimmering in tune, where we played happily; where Pop balanced his ginger moustache on his lipped granddad cup* and where the budgie once dived into Judy's soft Labrador mouth, which closed and opened so Bluey could soar again. Yet in growing shadows, the back gate opened every afternoon at 3pm, high heels clattered over the yard, and the latch clicked, but nobody was to be seen. The air sparked and frazzled. We always caught the next bus home.

As a child, I longed to stay the night with Hilary, but when allowed to sleep-over, repeated old patterns. I always cried to go home at 9 o'clock as the grey bedroom shadows sizzled, feeding my fears of nothingness...
60 years later, snugly camped on Hilary's sofa in Edgewater, we retold the stories, and heard old voices with new words: the only people left to share those times. I remembered I was a scaredy-cat, crying for home. Hilary told me how she was nightly terrified in her bedroom; a blocked off half-glazed door led to an unopened corridor to unused Maltings' offices, creaking, wood-clicking with scaring bangs. She would comfort my grizzling, and scream "Sheila wants to go home."
"Do you remember them scraping the ice, winding the starter motor and us bundled in the back, tumbling without seat belts."
" I can feel the fringe of the blanket, soft, reassuring. It was red with black and yellow stripes."
We were both lost in time, "No, it was red. Do you remember…". We had rocked asleep to the car's rhythm.

Back in Crystal Close, Edgewater, we remembered. Snapshots. Hilary recalled learnt country ways, competent at plucking and gutting a chicken at 5 years old, firmly earth-rooted. We remembered rocky road trips to timeless Pinnacles, to Stonehenge, trawling with our own children through Chesil beach, which squirrels rocks from every place in the world,,,and breaking open fossils in Kimmeridge Bay, Dorset, seeking pathways to the past.

* *Hilary's Grandad, "Pop" Edward Stannard was the local hero. First he was awarded an MBE for digging dynaminte out of a burning railway embankment during the war. Then in 1953, as the flood waters rose around Railway Cottages, Edward strode out, water up to his hips and re-leased the sows from the pigstys so that they could swim to higher land. Then Pop and Nan stood on the bedsprings while the water rose to their chests before the tide turned and rescue boats arrived. He was always calm in a crisis.*

Hilary driving the mini to Cornwall in teenage years, both mini skirted and carefree. We remembered house-sitting and ganneting a whole year's supply of Auntie Elsie's cherry pies in one weekend. We also sought deeper meanings. Stepping over the borderline, I retraced my Australian journey towards 14,000 year old handprints in Red-hands cave, where I heard silence whistle in the gap in time between two rock columns, when sound stopped and echoed the swirling of the years.

Next, we told the latest stories, of both of us coping with cancer. Hilary, 2 years before, poisoned with toxic red chemotherapy, which killed off her immunity, but also eventually the cancer. "No hair, ballooning with steroids, all I needed was tattoos and piercings." Phone chatting at that time, I had been terrified of her death, whilst Hilary was overwhelmed by the cure. The phone always rang softly, her voice cut in and out, a stalling engine spluttering in long-distance fibre-optics. " I couldn't bond with Liam at the time. I was too ill, too remote to hold my grandson." The undercurrents had nearly tugged my friend away. Now Liam clambers on his beloved grandma's lap, snuggles in, and listens to her stories of long ago and far away. Hilary gives glimpses into other lives and places, another realm.

 Hugging goodbye at the airport, I smiled through glazed eyes, fearful of never seeing my friend again, afraid I might discover myself lost and tuneless in the borderlands.

Back home. A letter fell from the overladen cupboard from the Borderlands, written by Hilary, when my dad died, in 1987, "This life is the hard bit, the illusion. He is in the real living now. Do you think they are talking hind legs off donkeys and I wonder how they think we turned out. Me, not too well I think. I wish we could have been flies on celestial walls when they started talking".

My friend Hilary knows how to keep in touch. When Hilary and family emigrated, I mourned and sought her in silent photos and voiceless films. Yet we have met at least every 7 years and in talking face to face, relished soft warm rhythms and built new myths.

Mothers and Daughters: Sheila, Jenny, Hilary, Rachel

67: Sheila in Hospital Land

Seven doctors in fourteen days, all
confidently re-confirmed my old diagnosis
"Rheumatoid Arthritis, nothing else wrong."
'Beware of labels, they cloud the mind.'
Left arm stopped moving, then the right leg.
You do the Hokey-Cokey, and can't turn about.
Can't walk now, in a wheelchair, stuck.
Doctor number eight spots my downhill slide.
opens the door into the hospital game.

(Where am I.? That's the great puzzle..)
"Why am I in a geriatric ward?"
"It's not, dear." replied the starched nurse.
"My mother in law of 93, slept in this bed.
The air is frusty, we're old and bedraggled."
"No we changed the name to muddle you more
Now we're the topsides-turkey specialist ward.
You are an enigma, a puzzle in the game.
You need a diagnosis to join in.
To win, you must move ward again."

My fellow gamesters are a motley team.
Mrs. Bhatacharee, right leg strung up high,
tended all day by three dutiful daughters
who crush pills to swallow in mango yoghurt.
Irish Mary from Clacton is forgotten,
six weeks in the same bed, no visitors,
Lived alone, marooned in a top floor flat,
no family to fight her corner, ignored.
Needs a spinal-op, but the London-specialist
Is too busy to assess the voiceless patient.
Doctors visits are rare, but the nurses care.
Mary smiles, chats, enjoys hospital company.

Beautiful Brenda with styled hair, painted face,
spends time mirror grooming to hide the truth.
Her family know about her breathing, not the MS.
We share our stories to ease our pain.

All night, Mrs. Bhatacharee chants prayers.
Mary, bent double, crawls to the loo on all fours,
Brenda drowses in tear stained disarray.
I am lying on the ceiling staring down.
Stray cats chase around the ward,
stopping only for polite conversation.
I am frightened. I ring for the commode.

"Who in the world am I? This is the great question"

Crack-cocaine Wayne yells in the corridor,
"I left my baby in the car. I want my mother."
All night long, the student nurse reassures,
"You've overdosed. You need to stay."
Head bang, knock the ward doors down.

How long is forever? Sometimes just one second.

The doctor looks quizzical.
I'm afraid I can't explain myself.
I'm not myself you see

"Six weeks ago, I could walk round London,
Somethings very wrong."

"My dear, here we must run as fast as we can,
Just to stay in the same place.
And if you want to go anywhere
You must run twice as fast as that."

"But I can't run anywhere, I'm stuck in the bed."

"You've cracked the puzzle, you're logical, not mad.
You're lucid. You win MRI scans for your wit.".

Wheelchaired to the X-ray waiting room,
Wayne and I twitch each side of the burly security man.
Wayne's swollen black saucer eyes swivel blankly.

    "But I don't want to be among mad people."
    "Oh you can't help that" said Wayne
    "We're all mad here. I'm mad, you're mad."

Frozen, I jitter-bug to the scanner's thunder.
A handsome registrar diagnoses me.
"Not a brain tumour." But I smile too soon,
"Considerable damage to your neck and spine.
Put this collar on, don't get out of bed.
If you sneeze, you could be paralysed.
Off to the best neck surgeon in Ipswich."
At midnight an ambulance crew steal me away.
My fellow players wish me well with envy.
First to leave. Did I win the game or lose?
My ambulance crew debate the best road,
puzzled as the Orwell Bridge is closed

    "If we don't know where we're going
    Any road can take us there."

(Indents thanks to Lewis Carroll)

68: Locked doors

Part one: The ritual
"Have you locked the backdoor, Dorian?"
Followed by teeth brushing, toileting,
tea swallowing, and Sudoku solving,
rituals to relax and ground myself.
Lights out, goodnight kiss, snuggle.
"Are you sure the door is locked?"
Unresolved fears surface, worries worm,
old jumble clutters up my brain.
Windows rattle, floor boards creak,
I tiptoe downstairs, test the handle.
Back door locked. Reassured,

Part two: The ritual broken
April 2016, sofa sleeping downstairs,
body failing, can't walk, can't work.
Not even able to crawl upstairs.
Back door checked. Safe,
from intruders, not from anxiety.
I avoid sleep oblivion, and listen.
Our cat flap is a super highway. All night
stray robber cats break in and enter,
scoop up Mog's scraps and scarper.

Part three: The ritual exposed
Next, diagnosis of compressed spinal chord.
Midnight ambulance to Ipswich hospital.
Ambulance staff cajole the door dragon,
"We're new here, we're from Essex.
We forgot our passports." Humour opens doors.
"Just once then, this is not the proper entrance."
Trolley clatter through a corridor labyrinth.
"Where is George Clooney when you need him?"
A warm welcome, a new ward world.

"Wriggle your toes," rectal examinations,
my feet feather-tickled, stick-scratched
"Close your eyes, which is which?"
Hourly neuro-tests to check my reflexes.
I respond, the clock hasn't stopped yet.

All night, I keep myself awake, present.
observant, frightened, unable to move.
A shadow tree waves on the blinds,
etched on my brain for eternity,
skeletal Spring branches whisper of change.
I picture my ancestors: Emily and George
Bessie, Flo, Millie. Ella, Elsie, Joan and Frank,
"It's not time to meet them yet."
2am. "Anyone need some morphine?"
Bells call, life dances around bed-pans.
4am. An ancient Suffolk voice grates the air,
"Barry, Barry, shut the front door.
I'm freezing, there's a draught."
A nurse comforts her, "Don't worry Sheila.
I'll shake up your pillow. Try to sleep."
A twin Sheila, I'd found my alter-ego.
All night Suffolk Sheila door-frets.
mirrors my illogical night-time fears.
Had I transformed into a batty old lady?

Part four: The ritual discarded?
At 5am, my consultant arrives, reassures.
Six surgeons operate for six hours,
replace my upper spine with metal discs.
Half shaved head, I survived,
slowly used my fingers, could text,
learnt to walk with a frame.
Healed now, rarely do I back door worry,
Suffolk Sheila demonstrated a cautionary story.
But nightly Dorian double rattles the door,
to dispel any remnants of my paranoia.

69: Lost and found in mirror time

Lost and found in mirror time,
my past and present reflections
jostle to grab my attention.
A baby touches her laughing friend,
cold, flat, smooth, hidden in glass.
A toddler with half chopped hair
stares out, guilty scissors in hand.
Six year old with gappy front teeth,
hopes for a magic fairy sixpence.
Pop star poster reflections compose
dreams and fears of teenage love.
Back combed hair, eyes kohl lined,
a student, I rebel to find true self,
"What is the meaning of life?"

Lost and found in mirror time.
Shouts echo from my sinful mirror, as
my mother destroys my hidden pills.
A hopeful bride peers, hair pieces
adorned with isolated white blooms.
Tear smudged mascara, return
to a single life of readjustment.

Lost and found in mirror time.
Rushed middle life, no time to stare.
Blow dry hair, daily make up rush.
Lover, mother, teacher, clogger,
Parents lost, no longer a daughter.
Learner, dreamer, traveller, searcher.
Distorted image, one breast less,
an Amazon warrior, survivor.
A bride dancing again at 50,
chemo thin hair under brimmed hat.
Cambridge degree gained at 60

A Counsellor holding a mirror for others,
too busy for my mirror self, ignored.
Lost in the midnight landing mirror,
a startled stranger stares out,
post-op, hair half shaved,
shocked dark rimmed eyes,
bent shoulders, shrunken neck.
Ignore this intruder, hurry past.
Rest, heal, mend, rebuild.

Found in the ageing mirror of time,
acceptance of a storm-weathered face:
well worn russet apple peel skin,
hair coloured to disguise my age,
forehead scar hidden under fringe,
Smile lines etched at mouth corners,
worry lines at bridge of nose,
under eye bags, big enough
for half of Sainsbury's.
Eye liner, mascara still applied.
Smile for reassurance, loses years.
My mirror friend reflects my smile,
affirms my self, mourns shared loss,
knows everything and nothing

Sheila Kelly and Val Taylor deep in research

Postscript 1

Mystery of the move from Horsted Keynes to Essex

Understanding why William Field decided to uproot his family in 1881 from Sussex to the banks of the River Stour in north-east Essex is problematic. Did financial difficulties at Little Oddynes, where he was gamekeeper, force his move? Why move such a large family so far away from all their relatives and family support? Travel was easier with the arrival of the railways, but what was the attraction of such a faraway new home?

Possible Reason for Uprooting the Family
My mother was told by her grandmother, Emily Field, that the family left because her father, William Field knew too much about a fire on the farm, and was forced to move away. However newspaper reports for Little Oddynes Farm only show a haystack fire on 29 August 1892, quickly extinguished, when Horsted Keynes was noted for excellent water supply. Later reports indicate a suspicious fire, 15 years after the move in 1896, suggesting the farm was in serious trouble.

Fire at Little Oddynes Farm. *14 July 1896, Mid Sussex Times.*
Fire in the barn at Little Oddynes farm, tenant of which is Mrs. Emma Hoadley. In the barn were about 60 trusses of straw, 10 trusses of hay, and a number of farming implements. The building was quickly in flames.
The Hayward's Heath fire brigade was telegraphed for, but not possessing an engine, they could not go as a brigade. The Captain (Mr. Golding) and some of the members journeyed to Horsted Keynes as quickly as possible, and a bucket brigade organised. Water, although not abundant, was obtained from the pond. The barn and three outbuildings were totally destroyed. Cause of the outbreak is not ascertained.
Mrs. Hoadley's son left the barn with some calves about 10 minutes, before the discovery of the fire; but he states he did not use the end of the barn, where the fire started, in which the straw was stacked and did not use a match in it.
The contents of the barn and outhouses are covered by insurance.

William Field probably moved, because of the farm's difficulties after the death in 1881 of John Hoadley, aged 76, owner of Oddynes Farm. Half of the farm was sold at auction by the executors on 19th August, with 'Valuable live and dead farming stock. Household furniture and effects.' Little Oddynes had financial problems, and would not have required a full time gamekeeper. Plus John Hoadley's son Edward, who inherited Little Oddynes seems unreliable. Edward died on October 1st 1889, after falling from a cart after 3 hours drinking at the Gardeners Arms. His wife, Emma inherited the farm. Soon after the fire in 1896, the Hoadleys gave up farming.

The mystery remains of why William moved his family so far. Further research at West Sussex record office could reveal new clues. Family history research is an ongoing quest into the past.

Postscript 2:
Lost on Southern Region: One Grandfather

Grandads were unknown creatures in my childhood: Joan and Frank never mentioned their fathers, when I was small. But slowly, my grandfathers' shameful stories emerged.

Walter Watson, my paternal grandfather, was an untrained dentist, from Bury St Edmunds, who in 1910 married Nell Harland, a waitress in the station cafe. Walter hit the bottle after his wife died in 1936, A cousin described how, on visits to the dental practice, Walter's hands shook so much that, before drilling, Walter gulped a secret brandy for steadiness. Walter was even on trial twice, for killing patients by using cocaine as an anaesthetic, instead of the proscribed medication. Frank moved to Manningtree to escape his drunken father. Walter was rescued from the Salvation Army Hostel in Derby by a rich widow, who married Walter. They attended Frank and Joan's wedding in 1940, but were not seen again before Walter died in 1950

William Aldridge Joan eventually gave some clues about her father William Aldridge, when I asked why her middle name 'Aldridge' was so peculiar. 'My mother Bessie never married my father. When she died, my father wanted to adopt me. But my grandparents wouldn't let him." William was apparently a manager on Southern Region Railway. In 1940, Joan described William as deceased on her marriage certificate, probably for convenience.

After I started researching family history in 1997, I spent 20 years looking for records about William Aldridge, but to no avail. I reasoned that William Aldridge was an uncommon name, and would be quickly found on railway employment records (on line in Ancestry). Occupation records revealed that 28 William Aldridges worked on Southern Region. After ruling out William Aldridges too young or too old to father Joan in 1918, a ridiculous 16 possibilities were left. Any could have been a possible grandad! But none were managers (maybe William lied about his status).

Probate records for at least 37 William Aldridge's who died in Kent, Sussex and London between 1919 to 1940 provided no links. None left any money to my mother.

Next I looked through WW1 military records for William Aldridge's who had worked on the railways. I found fishmongers, labourers, box-cutters, saddlers, drapers, bricklayers, blacksmiths and painters. No railway workers.

By 2015, I was disenchanted, and turned my attention to writing about my mother's family in Mistley. A family that I knew and loved. Oral stories, memories, photos, postcards and recipes held far more life than a list of possible railway employees names.

 DNA tests could provide a missing link to my grandfather, and in November 2019 Ancestry had a special offer. I hoped for first cousins to emerge from my mother's possible half siblings, even photos of William Aldridge, resplendent in Army or railway uniform. The test involved much bubbly spitting in a tube, far removed from family links. I waited for the results in trepidation, but my spit was not good enough! I had to repeat the test, and again waited anxiously to find my grandfather.

At last a breakthrough. One 4th cousin, with shared DNA, had Aldridge as her middle name, shared her tree with me, and revealed that her father was another Aldridge, who did not marry her mother in the 1920s. Although, not William this time. Apparently not a reliable family. The Aldridge family came from Hoddesdon, Hertfordshire, with many Williams through many generations, but none were railway employees. She found one possible link: Charles William Aldridge born in Hoddesdon in 1876, but at this moment, my 4th cousin has not found a direct link to the many Aldridge's on her tree branch.

Charles William Aldridge creates an enigma, as William is not his first name. Did everyone call him William, or did he intend to deceive Bessie when he told her his name? Charles Aldridge's father James was a bricklayer. His mother died in 1888, when he was 12 and the family moved in with his grandmother by 1891, with younger siblings Ellen 9 and 2 year old Willie. Charles went into the army, the Dorset Regiment, which seems strange for a lad from Hertfordshire. On 10 May 1905, Charles became a painter at London Bridge

Station. He married Ellen Sprules in 1907. By the 1911 census Charles was a railway porter, and they lived at 10 Goodwood Road, New Cross, and had no children. Charles William Aldridge rejoined the Dorset Regiment in December 1915. Charles and Ellen were still living in Goodwood Road in the wartime census of September 1939, only a few months before Joan's wedding.

I need to try and prove a DNA link with Charles William Aldridge. At present he is the most likely Hoddesdon grandad. As more people take DNA tests, further links will hopefully emerge. Another William Aldridge, a railway manager, might emerge from the shadows. For now, I need to search for all possible links with Aldridge ancestors of my 237 distant DNA cousins. So far, most of my DNA cousins seem to be from Bessie's mother Emily's ten brothers and sisters.

My grandfather, William Aldridge, might never be found, and remain hidden in a railway siding on the Southern Region forever.

Postscript 3:

Workhouse Jottings

Bessie's employment at Tendring Workhouse in 1919, was in a period of significant change in workhouse organisation. Boards of Guardians were now appointed by local councils, and included women and working class representatives. Treatment of inmates slowly became less punitive, and more caring. In Tendring the changes were resisted by the old master and pre-war guardians. People continued to fear going into the spike.

Newspaper cuttings show the inequalities in the treatment between 'deserving' poor and supposedly 'undeserving', and the general reluctance to spend money by the Guardians. In 1922, the Master of Tendring described vagrants as *'carriers of fleas and disease....such humbugs must be segregated, to give a chance to the decent fellows, who are genuinely in search of work."*

Profits of £60-7s-9d were made on pigs in the Union-house during the last half year. *28 October 1911.*
(The Guardians were reluctant to authorise pork for Christmas lunch. In 1912 Henry Burton, workhouse master, announced *" a pig has died from a fit, caused by over eating."* Reverend Beadel quipped *"Extra care should be taken that the inmates do not over-indulge.")*

Burglary Tendring workhouse premises had been burglariously entered, access being gained over the roof behind the boardroom. The food cupboard of the male officers mess room was completely cleared out. 31 March 1911.

Coronation Tendring Guardians have decided to allow all old people in receipt of outdoor relief an extra 1s, and 6d for each child on the occasion of the Coronation 12 May 1911.

Lunatics Tendring Guardians resolved that in future lunatics be removed to the Asylum by motor car instead of rail to avoid painful scenes in public. 10 May 1913

Cottage home The inspectors report stated there were 49 children in the workhouse.1911, including 7 with widowed fathers, 9 deserted by parents, 5 orphans, 2 'mentally defective' and 10 children of unmarried mothers.-The House Committee reported that a cottage home for school age children should be built at once. The Guardians purchased grounds some years ago. The

Guardians voted by 21 votes to 4 that the Board do not feel justified in incurring the additional expense. 2 January 1914. (The Firs and The Limes Cottage for children were not built until 1920)

Elderly and Infirm

In October 1913, an enquiry was carried out by the British Board of Nursing after Guardian, Mrs. Hooper, was thwarted by the other Tendring Guardians when she requested

> *1) that the aged, sick and dying in the Infirmary should be supplied with soft feather pillows,*
>
> *2) that instead of iron enamelled mugs there shall be China mugs, and*
>
> *3) in case a patient needs attention there should be a bell at the side of each bed."*

The British Journal of Nursing November 1st 1913 rejected complaints that Mrs. Hooper interfered by steadying and offering a drink to a patient, nearly falling out of bed

> *"We are of the opinion that the infirmary is understaffed with trained nurses. The present staff only provides for one trained nurse to supervise the care of sixty patients in fourteen wards, day or night. It is the duty of the Guardians to provide sufficient skilled care for the sick in their charge ....We regret that the Guardians failed to support Mrs. Hooper's resolution, and hope their platitudinous pronouncements be rescinded, ...and a system of nursing be adopted to secure the patients a standard at once sufficient, efficient and humane.*
>
> *Until which time we repeat "POOR OLD PEOPLE."*

Staff Recruitment

Recruitment and retention of staff was difficult because of isolation, especially in winter. The nearest station was 4 miles away at Weeley. Guardians were out of touch with the problem,even refusing to provide a piano for female staff in 1911. Again in 1914, the workhouse master stressed it was difficult for nurses to know how to fill the long empty evenings. Chairman Rev. Beadel replied, *"as compared with other workhouses, it had greater comfort, and staff should be thankful to remain."*

Outings

An annual outing to Clacton was provided for the inmates, by motor coach in 1914. After a look around, inmates had a dinner of 'hot and cold lamb, beer, new potatoes, salad, fruit tarts, custard." In the afternoon inmates had free entrance to the Pier and Picture Palace, granted by a piece of calico with the word Tendring printed on, pinned under coat collars or inside cuffs. Tea of bread, butter and shrimps was provided, with a bowl of strawberries for the old ladies, whilst the old men were given an ounce of tobacco. The outings were suspended during the war.

World War One

Lack of consideration for the welfare of the inmates and penny pinching continued throughout and beyond World War One. Staff shortages caused extra problems in the war. In April 1915 many national newspapers reported the response to a call for workmen for the munitions factories:

"Tendring board of Guardians have only three officers left, in addition to the master, viz a stoker with one arm, a porter with one leg, and an invalid out of the navy."

Several boys were hired out from the workhouse because of shortages of land workers. Their wages were probably paid directly to the Workhouse!

The former cook left in 1914 to be trained as a nurse. The post was advertised at £35 per year, but becoming a workhouse cook was not an attractive proposition in the war when women were eager to support the war effort,

Some of the Guardians strongly supported dietary restrictions and cost savings because of wartime food shortages. Sugar rations were cut for staff and adult inmates.

"In 1914, about one and half tons of sugar were used, and after economies were introduced it saved the Workhouse in a full year, half a ton of sugar or 5oz. per inmate.

Reverend Beadel remarked *"the inmates must try to do without to help out...he knew the inmates were fond of sugar, but other people in better circumstances had given up sugar in their tea."*

In 1917, a second meatless day was ordered, when the inmates had cheese and bread instead of meat, though the elderly could continue with their normal meat diet (often beef stock). Budgetary constricts meant that substitutes like oatmeal were often used, and fish served twice a week instead of once. Bessie became cook in 1919, when there were still some shortages, but normality was returning. However, whilst some of the Guardians supported improvements, others wanted a more punitive approach to continue.

Last minute news

Authors and readers of reconstructed family history BEWARE!

At any moment your family memoir can be destabilised by newly found evidence. Research never stops: we are enmeshed in ever evolving stories.

Yesterday I delighted in my first proof copy of "Searching for Bessie" enjoying making the last small edits ("recipes" keep trying to change themselves to "recipies")

Then an email from Ancestry arrived with a possible baptism entry for my mother from newly computerised London parish records.

I had searched carefully through Mistley parish records in the past but could find no record of Joan's baptism.

Joan was baptised on January 1, 1919 but not at Mistley Church. Her baptism was at Saint Anne's Brondesbury near Kilburn, and Bessie's address was given as 20 Victoria Road. This means after release from Queen Charlotte's hospital on December 17th 1918, Bessie had returned to the unmarried mothers' hostel in Kilburn.

 As historian I should immediately delete Chapter 32: Christmas Eve 1918. Bessie did not return home with Joan for Christmas, She did not make mince and apple pies with Elsie or orange cream. By contrast, mother and sisters probably trod on eggshells to avoid mentioning her and Joan in front of George while missing Bessie.

But as Bessie's granddaughter and storyteller, I am concerned for her distress. It is impossible to provide a happy ever after ending, but I have decided to leave Bessie at home for her last Christmas enveloped in love by her mothers and sisters.

As varied readers you will have different reactions to me giving Bessie a happy Christmas.

Bessie was welcomed home, but not for Christmas celebrations. My Auntie Elsie often told the story of Bessie's homecoming, (Chapter 31) but this actually happened in early 1919.

Baptism solemnized in the Parish of St. Anne, Brondesbury
in the Diocese of London
County of Middlesex — in the Year One thousand
nine hundred and Eighteen & nineteen.

Alleged Date of Birth	When Baptised	Child's Christian Name.	Parents' Names. Christian.	Surname.	Abode.	Quality, Trade or Profession.	By whom the Ceremony was performed.
7.11.18	22nd November 1918. No. 649	Angus Gordon	Agnes Mabel	Whitear	20. Victoria Road.	—	R. Everard Blake.
8.12.17	24th November 1918. No. 650	John Francis Newton	Gerald Francis & Minnie Matilda	Weston	3. Dunmore Road.	Printer	R. Everard Blake.
15.12.18	1st January 1919 No. 651	Elsie Hayton	Emma	Cooper	20 Victoria Road	Domestic Servant	Franks. Morgan
8.12.18	1st January 1919 No. 652	Joan Aldridge	Bessie Emma	Reason	20 Victoria Road	Domestic servant	Franks S. Morgan
2.1.19	17th January 1919 No. 653	Florence Herrington	Louisa	Piggie	20 Victoria Road	Waitress	Franks S. Morgan
29.12.18	17th January 1919 No. 654	Hilda Marjorie	Emily	Searle	20 Victoria Road	Linen-keeper	Frank S. Morgan
26.12.18	22 Jan. 1919 No. 655	Allen Scott	Eleanor	Thistleton	20 Victoria Road	Domestic servant	Franks S. Morgan.
7.11.19	28th Feb 1919 No. 656	Gladys Violet	Charles Frederick & Lily Louisa	Peoks	24. Douglas Road.	Provision Salesman	R. Everard Blake
8.3.19	19th March 1919 657	Walter John	Lilian Violet	Perfect	Witherley Lane, Beaconsfield	Domestic servant	Frank S. Lloyd

260

Saint Anne's Church in Brondesbury frequently baptised babies from 20 Victoria Road. In 1918 and 1919, babies of single mothers formed 70% of the baptisms in the church. Many mothers entered the father's surname as the baby's middle name - as with Joan Aldridge Reason. By 1920 soldiers had returned from the trenches and only 20% of the baptisms at Saint Anne's were with residents of 20 Victoria Road.

Bibliography

Ancestry: http://www.ancestry.co.uk

Army Catering Corps: Manual of Army Catering Services (1965)

Cleveland, David: Mistley and Manningtree (Malthouse Press, Suffolk, 2017)

Cox, Pam: Servants (TV series, BBC4, 2012)

Duckworth, Jeannie: Fagin's Children, (Hambledon and London 2002)

Find My Past: findmypast.com

Fountain, Nigel: Women at War, (Imperial War Museum)

Fowler, Simon: The Workhouse (Pen and Sword History,2014)

Gould, J.M: The Women's Corps: the establishment of women's military services in Britain.   http:// www. discovery:culture.ac.uk 1988)

Halifax,Stuart: Citizens at War: the Experience of the Great War in Essex   (Queens College, Oxford, 2010)

Higginbotham, Peter: The Workhouse Cookbook (History Press, 2008)

Higginbotham, Peter: Voices from the Workhouse (History Press, 2012)

Bob Horlock: Visiting the Past: Images of Misley, Manningtree and Lawford, (Self Published)

Humphries, Steve and Gordon, Pamela: A Labour of Love (Sidgwick and Jackson, 1993)

James T. McKay: The Spike: A history of Tendring Workhouse, (Thesis 1990)

Phillips, Andrew: Colchester in the Great War (Pen and Sword Books, 2017)

Rickwood, Ken: Stour Secrets (David Cleveland, 2008)

Scutzenburger, Anne Ancelin: The Ancestor Syndrome (Routledge 1998)

Shipton, Elizabeth: Female Tommies (The History Press, 2014)

THANKS TO:

Dorian Kelly for his constant support and encouragement, publishing and computer skills.

Val Taylor for days spent with me remembering family stories, and exploring her photo chest.

Petra McQueen for editing 'Searching for Bessie' and her inspirational Creative Writing classes with The Writers' Company (contact@thewriterscompany.co.uk) and the WEA. I value her creative encouragement. Also to my fellow class-mates' positive support, enthusiasm and suggestions.

Red Lion Books, Colchester, for advice, friendship and encouragement

Patrick Denny and Andrew Philips for sharing their enthusiasm for local and family history and for teaching me valuable research skills.

London Metropolitan Archives, and **Essex Record Office** for their friendly guidance in finding old records.

My cousins, **Ann Smith** (Rene and Ron's daughter), and her sister **Janet Fox** (Who sadly died from Covid-19 in February 2021), **Pauline Atkinson (**Evelyn and George's daughter), **Mandy Rose Taylor,** (Val and Geoff's daughter) and **Carolyn Reid,** (Eileen and Geoff's daughter) for sharing memories and photos, and their good company over the years.

The family pattern of girls forming the majority of births continued into the next generation. Great-grandfather George Reason probably muttering "Not another old girl" in his grave!

My friends **Sally Tarpey, Margaret Colyer,** and **Jane Gaddas** for reading sections, commenting and encouraging me.

All my friends and family for their love and encouragement throughout my life.

Warning!

The recipes in this book
have not been tested
for a hundred years!

Please cook with a
sense of adventure..

For my cousin
Val Taylor,
our family
storyteller

and for my
daughter, .
Jenny Light
to meet her
ancestors

with much love

165 Cheese Baston	136. Rice Buns
166 General Bulletin	137 Curates Pudding
167 Dried Apricot Jam (h.l.)	138 Golden Pudding
168 Cheese Biscuits	139 College Pudding
169 Cheese Fritters	140 Ginger bread Cake
110 Fluffy Cakes	141 Strawberry Cream
111 Roman Pie	142 Hot Cross buns
112 Tenderous of Fish of chicken	143 Biscuits
113 Savoury Anchovies	144 Walnut Cake
114 Savoury Souffles	145 Fruit Cake
115 Cheese Tartlets	146 Turkish Delight
116 Neapolitan Cutlets	147 Green Tomato Pickle
117 Fish Mould	148 Christmas Pudding
118 Lemon Curd	149 Norfolk Short Cake
119 Jam Sandwich	150 Chocolate Sauce
120 Lemon Jelly	151 Cheese Straws
121 Eggs au Gratin	152 Ginger Cake
122 Ruby Pudding	153 Tea Biscuits
123 Sponge Cake	154 Uncle Toms Pudding
124 Lemon Curd	155 Cornish Splits
125 Chocolate Cakes	156 Tomato Eggs
126 Floating Islands	157 Rhubarb Jam
127 Almond Biscuits	158 Water Biscuits
128 Fish Souffle	159 Violet Cake
129 Brandy Snaps	160 Sponge Cakes
130 Plum Cake	161 Short Bread
131 Yorkshire Tea Cakes	162 Rice Omelet
132 Cornflour Cakes	163 Marie Pudding
133 Mincemeat	164 Sago Figgers
134 Chocolate Eclairs	165 Delight Cake
135 Borshock Soup	166 Kidney Beans
	167 Kidney Beans
	168 Fish Cake
	169 Chocolate Souffle
	170 Gold Slice
	171 Lemon Sponge
	172 Potato Mousse
	173 Biscuity
	174 Vinegar Cake